The Metaphysical Theory of the State

Originally published in 1918, this enduring work by renowned sociologist and Liberal politician Leonard Trelawny Hobhouse encompasses a series of five key lectures, first delivered at the London School of Economics in the autumn of 1917. Outlining Hobhouse's theories on social investigation, freedom, law and the will of the state, this edition revives an important work, which has long been unavailable.

T0352768

The Metaphysical Theory of the State
A Criticism

L. T. Hobhouse

Routledge
Taylor & Francis Group

First published in 1918
by George Allen & Unwin Ltd

This edition first published in 2009 by Routledge
2 Park Square, Milton Park, Abingdon, Oxon, OX14 4RN

Simultaneously published in the USA and Canada
by Routledge
605 Third Avenue, New York, NY 10017

Routledge is an imprint of the Taylor & Francis Group, an informa business

Publisher's Note
The publisher has gone to great lengths to ensure the quality of this reprint but
points out that some imperfections in the original copies may be apparent.

Disclaimer
The publisher has made every effort to trace copyright holders and welcomes
correspondence from those they have been unable to contact.

ISBN 13: 978-0-415-55275-2 (hbk)
ISBN 13: 978-0-415-55786-3 (pbk)
ISBN 13: 978-0-203-87127-0 (ebk)

THE METAPHYSICAL
THEORY *of the* STATE

SOCIAL DEVELOPMENT:
ITS NATURE AND CON-
DITIONS

THE RATIONAL GOOD:
A STUDY IN THE LOGIC
OF PRACTICE

ELEMENTS OF SOCIAL
JUSTICE

———————◆———————

BY J. A. HOBSON AND MORRIS GINSBERG

L. T. HOBHOUSE: HIS LIFE
AND WORK

THE METAPHYSICAL THEORY
OF THE STATE

A Criticism

By

L. T. HOBHOUSE

London
GEORGE ALLEN & UNWIN LTD
Ruskin House Museum Street

FIRST PUBLISHED IN 1918
SECOND IMPRESSION 1922
THIRD IMPRESSION 1926
FOURTH IMPRESSION 1938
FIFTH IMPRESSION 1951

PRINTED IN GREAT BRITAIN
BY PHOTOTYPE LTD. LONDON

DEDICATION

TO LIEUTENANT R. O. HOBHOUSE, R.A.F

My Dear Oliver,

If you can carry your memory across the abyss which separates us all from July 1914, you will remember some hours which we spent reading Kant together in a cool Highgate garden in those summer days of peace. I think by way of relaxation we sometimes laid aside Kant, took up Herodotus, and felt ourselves for a moment in the morning of the world. But it is of Kant that I remind you, because three years later I was reading his great successor in the same garden in the same summer weather, but not with you. One morning as I sat there annotating Hegel's theory of freedom, jarring sounds broke in upon the summer stillness. We were well accustomed to the noises of our strange new world that summer. Daily if the air was still we heard, as some one said, the thud of guns across the northern sea, and murmur of innumerable 'planes. But this morning it was soon clear that something more was on foot. Gunfire, at first distant, grew rapidly nearer, and soon broke out from the northern heights hard by. The familiar drone of the British aeroplanes was pierced by the whining of the Gothas. High above, machine guns barked in sharp staccato and distant thuds announced the fall of bombs.

Presently three white specks could be seen dimly through the light haze overhead, and we watched their course from the field. The raid was soon over. The three specks drifted away towards the east, the gunfire died down, the whining faded away, and below the hill the great city picked up its dead. The familiar sounds resumed their sway, the small birds chirruped from the shrubs, and the distant murmur of the traffic told of a world going steadily on its accustomed course.

As I went back to my Hegel my first mood was one of self-satire. Was this a time for theorizing or destroying theories, when the world was tumbling about our ears? My second thoughts ran otherwise. To each man the tools and weapons that he can best use. In the bombing of London I had just witnessed the visible and tangible outcome of a false and wicked doctrine, the foundations of which lay, as I believe, in the book before me. To combat this doctrine effectively is to take such part in the fight as the physical disabilities of middle age allow. Hegel himself carried the proof-sheets of his first work to the printer through streets crowded with fugitives from the field of Jena. With that work began the most penetrating and subtle of all the intellectual influences which have sapped the rational humanitarianism of the eighteenth and nineteenth centuries, and in the Hegelian theory of the god-state all that I had witnessed lay implicit. You may meet his Gothas in mid air, and may the full power of a just cause be with you. I must be content with more pedestrian methods. But " to make the world a safe place for democracy," the weapons of the spirit are as necessary as those of the flesh. You have described to me times when your lofty world is peaceable enough— above the Canal in the dawn, when all the desert lies gray and still before the first sunbeam sets the air moving, or alone in the blueness, cut off by a bank of cloud from earth. When at such times the mind works freely and you think over the meaning of the great contest, I should like to think that you carried with you some ideas from this volume to your heights. At any rate you will bear with you the sense that we are together as of old, in that in our different ways we are both fighters in one great cause.

Your affectionate father,

L. T. HOBHOUSE.

NOTE

THE substance of this volume was given in a course of lectures at the London School of Economics in the autumn of 1917.

I have to thank my colleague Dr. A. Wolf for reading the MS. and making several useful emendations of detail.

CONTENTS

APPENDIX

THE METAPHYSICAL THEORY
OF THE STATE

LECTURE I

THE OBJECTS OF SOCIAL INVESTIGATION

PEOPLE naturally begin to think about social questions
when they find that there is something going wrong in
social life. Just as in the physical body it is the ailment
that interests us, while the healthy processes go on without
our being aware of them, so a society in which everything
is working smoothly and in accordance with the accepted
opinion of what is right and proper raises no question
for its own members. We are first conscious of diges-
tion when we are aware of indigestion, and we begin to
think about law and government when we feel law to be
oppressive or see that government is making mistakes.
Thus the starting-point of social inquiry is the point at
which we are moved by a wrong which we desire to set
right, or, perhaps at a slightly higher remove, by a lack
which we wish to make good. But from this starting-
point reflection advances to a fuller and more general
conception of society. If we begin by criticizing some
particular injustice, we are led on to discuss what justice
is. Beginning with some special social disorder, we are
forced to examine the nature of social order and the
purposes for which society exists. The social theory
which we reach on these lines is a theory of ends, values,
purposes, which leads us up to Ethics or Moral Philosophy,
to questions of the rights and duties of man, and the
means by which institutions of society may be made to

conform thereto. The principles of Ethics are supreme, or, as they have been called, architectonic. They apply to man in all relations and to life on all sides. They guide, or are meant to guide, the personal life of man no less than his collective and political activities. They provide the standard by which all human relations are to be judged. When, therefore, we study social and political institutions with a view to ascertaining their value or justification, our inquiry is in reality a branch of Ethics. Our results rest in the end on the application of principles of well-being to the social organization of man. This is one perfectly legitimate method of social inquiry, and as involving an analysis of common experience, leading up to or down from a theory of ends or values, it is appropriately called Social Philosophy.

Legitimate as it is, this method of investigating society has its special danger. In pursuing the ideal it sometimes loses hold of the actual. In analysing the meaning of institutions it may overlook their actual working, and if we follow it too blindly we may end either in abstract propositions which have little relation to practical possibility and serve only to breed fanatics ; or in abandoning the interest in actual society altogether and amusing ourselves with the construction of Utopias. In reaction from this tendency many students would say that the primary business of social theory is to investigate the facts of social life as they are, the historical development of society and its several institutions, the statistical description of any given society as it is, the endeavour to ascertain the laws of cause and effect which, it is held, must permeate social life as they permeate every other sphere of reality. In place of a social philosophy, then, we have a social science, and it is held that by a social science we can ascertain, measure and predict, just as we can ascertain, measure and predict the behaviour of any system of physical bodies.

Without touching here on the question whether in social science prediction is possible or not, it is sufficient to say that the scientific study of social life or the endeavour to ascertain the relations of cause and effect is not only a legitimate object but one which has in point of fact yielded good results. Few would now deny that the strictly scientific method has its place in social inquiry. But objection may still be taken to the distinction between ideals and facts. To begin with, it may be urged that the social inquirer could not if he would lay aside his ideals. Whenever we are dealing with social life we are dealing with a matter of profound interest to ourselves. When the chemist wishes to ascertain the temperature at which a solid liquefies, or a liquid boils, he has in the end to read off a certain observation, and it is not a matter of profound human interest whether the figure that he reads is 150° or 160° ; but when a social student inquires how an institution is working, whether a new law is attaining its object, whether Trade Union activity is or is not succeeding in raising wages, shortening hours or otherwise improving the condition of the operatives, the answer to his question is not only in reality much more difficult to ascertain but is also one which stirs prejudices, confirms or refutes presuppositions, is certain to be challenged by lively interests. The difficulty is not peculiar to the study of contemporary fact. History, even ancient history, is written in a certain spirit and a certain temper dependent on the personal presuppositions of the writer. Human affairs are so complex and the interweaving of cause and effect so subtle that in the presentation of an historical development there will always be an element dependent on the point of view of the writer and on the selection and emphasis which may honestly seem the fairest selection and the natural emphasis to the particular writer, but which may seem quite other to a different investigator approaching the same object with a different background of thought.

Nor is this all. Putting aside all that may be said as to the bias of investigators, it may be urged that the subject of investigation itself is charged throughout with the ideals, emotions, interests of men and women, both as individuals and as corporate bodies ; and, moreover, the logic of those ideals, the very thing which social philosophy investigates, the degree, that is, of their mutual consistency or inconsistency, is a matter of profound importance to their actual working. If two ideals penetrate the same nation or the same class and those two ideals are at bottom in conflict, the results must show themselves in the tangle of history. They must manifest themselves in divided aims and ultimately in failure. If, on the other hand, they are coherent and harmonious, then once more that result must appear in the greatness of the success attending their historical development. Thus, if we start with the most rigid determination to adhere to facts, we shall find that ideals are a part of the facts, and if we say that nevertheless we will treat them as facts without examining their truth, we shall find it hard to adhere to that position because their consistency and coherence, which are intimately relevant to their truth, deeply affect their practical efficiency.

It may be granted that it is easier to distinguish the philosophical and the scientific treatment of society in principle than to keep them apart in practice. In principle we call the philosophical inquiry that which deals with the aim of life, with the standard of conduct, with all that ought to be, no matter whether it is or is not. The scientific method we call that which investigates facts, endeavours to trace cause and effect, aims at the establishment of general truths which hold good whether they are desirable or not. The distinction of principle is clear, but in point of fact the inquiry into ideals can never desert the world of experience without danger of losing itself in unreality and becoming that which the poet of idealism was unfairly called, " a beautiful, ineffectual angel beating in the void his luminous wings in vain." The ideal, though it has never been realized and perhaps may never be realized, must grow out of reality. It must be that which we can become, not that which is utterly removed from the emotions and aspirations which have grown up within us in the actual evolution of mind. The ethically right, Professor Höffding has said, must be sociologically possible. Thus, even as pure theory, the philosophical view cannot afford to disregard the facts. Still less can it do so if it passes over, as philosophy should, into the constructive attempt to reorganize life in accordance with its ideals. If the principles which it discovers are to be realized in this workaday world, this can only be by intimate knowledge of the details of this world, by the control of events through their causes, for the discovery of which we must go to pure science. Social Science, on the other hand, as we have seen, cannot ignore the elements of idealism as a working factor, as one of the forces, if you will, among the other forces, which it studies ; nor can it disregard the logical consistency or inconsistency of ideas, upon which their working force depends. Thus the philosophical, the scientific, and the practical interest, however distinct in theory, tend in their actual operation to be intermingled, and it must be admitted that we cannot carry one through without reference to the other.

Nevertheless, to keep the issues distinct at every point is the first necessity of sound reasoning upon social affairs. What is essential for social investigation, whether it starts with the philosophic or scientific interest, is that in putting any question it should know precisely what that question is ; specifically, whether it is a question of what is desirable, of what ought to be ; or a question of what has been, is, or probably will be. These two questions, though necessarily related, are no less necessarily distinct, and to confuse them is the standing temptation of the social inquirer. If the social philosopher has sometimes thought to legislate for society without first informing himself of the facts as to what is possible and what is not, the scientific sociologist on his side is not innocent of all encroachments. It is a standing temptation to overbear questions of right and wrong by confident predictions, which in reality rest more on the prepossessions of the prophet than on his insight into cause and effect.

It is the weakness of human nature that it likes to be on the winning side, and just as in an election the argument most effective in catching votes is the demonstration that we are winning already—a demonstration which might seem to make effort on that side superfluous—so in the study of social and economic development it is rhetorically effective to demonstrate that a particular social change is at hand, that it is an inevitable consequence of a concatenation of events that is bringing it about whether we will or not ; and this demonstration exercises, and is intended to exercise, a kind of coercion upon our minds whereby we resign ourselves to accept the change as desirable on the strength of arguments which have never touched its desirability at all, but have proved, if they have proved anything, nothing more than the probable effect of certain operative causes. Intellectually, this method is one of confusion ; morally, it is paralysing to the will. If there were nothing for us but to accept the trend of events as we find it, then our science would relapse into fatalism, and, as members of the society which we study, we should be in the position simply of knowing the course of the stream which carries us along without any increase in the power to guide it, whether it happen to be taking us into the haven or over Niagara.

When we allow Social Science thus to persuade us of the inevitableness of things, we are reversing the normal course of science. For, whatever else may be said of science, one of its functions is to increase human power, and this applies to sciences which deal with human life as well as to sciences which deal with inanimate objects. When we know the etiology of a disease we acquire for the first time a real prospect of controlling it. So it should be in social affairs, but so it can only be if we hold firmly to the distinction between the desirable and the actual, if we grasp clearly the principles which should regulate social life, and do not allow ourselves to be shaken in our hold of them by any knowledge of the changes which are actually going on among us. The foundation, therefore, of true social method is to hold the ideal and the actual distinct and use our knowledge of the one as a means to realizing the other. We may pursue the two investigations, if we will, side by side, for we have seen how very closely they are interwoven. But every question that we ask and every statement that we make ought to be quite clearly a statement as to fact or an assertion of what ought to be, and never a hybrid of the two.

This distinction would, I think, be accepted both by the bulk of ethical thinkers and of scientific students of society, but there exists a form of social theory which repudiates it in principle. The foundation of this theory is the belief that the ideal is realized in the actual world, and in particular in the world of organized society, not in the sense already noted above that there are ideals operating as psychological forces in human beings, but in the sense that the world at large, and in particular the social world, is, if properly understood, an incarnation or expression of the ideal ; that, as one thinker would put it, the Absolute is perfection ; or, as Hegel, who may be considered as the father of this school, laid down, " the insight to which . . . philosophy is to lead us is that the real world is as it ought to be." [1] The theory of society on this view is not to be detached from general metaphysics ; it is an integral part of the philosophy of things. Just as in a simple form of religion, the powers that be are ordained of God, so with the metaphysician who starts from the belief that things are what they should be, the fabric of human life, and in particular the state system, is a part of an order which is inherently rational and good, an order to which the lives of individuals are altogether subordinate. The problem of social theory upon this view will not consist in the formulation of ideals as distinct from anything actual, yet capable of becoming actual if once human beings grasp them with a very firm determination to realize them ; still less can it consist in investigating facts in distinction from

[1] *Philosophy of History,* p. 38.

ideals, for the very foundation of society as a part of the fabric of things is the ideal which it enshrines. The problem will be neither ethical nor scientific. It will start by a repudiation of the distinction upon which we have been insisting, and its task will be to state the nature of society in terms revealing the ideal elements which mere facts have a tendency to veil from our human eyes.

This, then, is the metaphysical theory of the state. It is the endeavour to exhibit the fabric of society in a light in which we shall see it, in or through its actual condition, as the incarnation of something very great and glorious indeed, as one expression of that supreme being which some of these thinkers call the Spirit and others the Absolute. There is no question here of realizing an ideal by human effort. We are already living in the ideal. It does not much matter whether we are rich or poor, healthy or enfeebled, personally aware of happiness or misery ; nay, it does not seem to matter very much whether we are just or unjust, virtuous or depraved, for we all are integral parts in something much wider and nobler than the individual life, something to which mere human good and evil, happiness or misery, are small matters, mere constituent elements that, whatever they may be for each one of us, play their part right well in the magnificent whole. Evil is indeed necessary to good. It is a part of the Perfection of the Absolute, and anything which would point to its extirpation as an ideal is condemned as an offshoot of popular notions of progress or ridiculed as a piece of humanitarian enthusiasm.

Such, then, is the spirit of the metaphysical theory of society which I propose to examine in the shape given to it by its founder, Hegel, and his most modern and most faithful exponent, Dr. Bosanquet. This theory is commonly spoken of as idealism, but it is in point of fact a much more subtle and dangerous enemy to the ideal than any brute denial of idealism emanating from a one-sided science. Against every attempt to construe the world as mere fact which we cannot modify, there will always spring up the reaction of human hope, of human endeavour, of the deep-seated indignation at injustice, the "rebel passion" of pity. If the scientific man insists that as this world rose out of the whirl of atoms, agitated by mechanical forces, so it will ultimately disappear in the cold and darkness, none the less men will say "Here are we, conscious living beings palpitating with emotion, with feeling, products it may be of your whirl of atoms, yet allowed meanwhile some latitude to shape our lives, to avoid the worst evils and to cultivate some fleeting happiness; let us at least stand together against this unkindly fate and make the best of life while we can, not only for our short-lived selves, but for our feeble race." Thus mechanical science stimulates at least the ethics of revolt. But when we are taught to think of the world which we know as a good world, to think of its injustices, wrongs and miseries as necessary elements in a perfect ideal, then, if we accept these arguments, our power of revolt is atrophied, our reason is hypnotized, our efforts to improve life and remedy wrong fade away into a passive acquiescence in things as they are; or, still worse, into a slavish adulation of the Absolute in whose hands we are mere pawns. These, it may be said, are questions of general rather than social philosophy, but the point is that to the idealistic school, social philosophy is an application of the theory of the Absolute to human affairs. As Dr. Bosanquet tells us,[1] "the treatment of the state in this discussion is naturally analogous to the treatment of the universe." The happiness of the state is not to be judged by the happiness of the individual; the happiness of the individual must be judged by the goodness of the state. It is to be valued by the perfection of the whole to which he belongs. In the conception, therefore, of the state as a totality, which is an end in itself, an end to which the lives of men and women are mere means, we have the working model of an Absolute. For the thoroughgoing idealist, all the conscious beings that live under the shadow of

[1] *The Principle of Individuality and Value*, p. 311.

the Absolute seem to have just as much or as little title to independent consideration as the cells of the human body. Now, for Hegel, the state is a form of the absolute spirit, which is the essence of all things. " The state is the divine idea as it exists on earth." [1] For " all the worth which the human being possesses— all spiritual reality he possesses only through the state." [2] " The state is the spirit which stands in the world and realizes itself therein consciously. . . . The existence of the state is God's movement in the world." [3] " The state is the divine will as the present spirit unfolding itself to the actual shape and organization of a world " (*Ph. d. R.* p. 327). " It is the absolute power upon earth " (p. 417). " It is its own end (*Selbst-zweck*). It is the ultimate end which has the highest right against the individual, whose highest duty is to be a member of the state " (p. 306).

The method followed by this theory is not ethical because it does not seek to find reasons for human conduct in any ultimate goal of human endeavour or in any rational principle of human duty. It does not seek these because it denies that the reflective reason of the individual is the method by which truth about ideals is to be ascertained. All true ideals are actual ; they belong to what is called the objective mind ; they are incarnated in the laws, traditions, customs of the society to which we belong. Nor, again, is the method scientific. It is neither historical nor statistical. It does not concern itself with the varying forms of social institutions, nor with the correlations of co-existence or succession. It assumes certain abstract conceptions [4] and expounds them dogmatically in general terms, putting aside the appeal to experience. If actual societies differ from the idealistic conception of them, so much the worse for

---

[1] *Philosophy of History*, E. T., p. 41.
[2] Ibid. p. 10 f.
[3] *Philosophie des Rechts*, pp. 312–13.
[4] Not that they are admitted to be abstract. They are believed by the idealist to be the very soul of reality (see, e.g., *Phil. des Rechts*, p. 58).

those societies. Thus the centre of discussion is "the state," as though there were precisely one and only one type of social organization to which the name applies and which can be described without reference to experience in universal terms. Dr. Bosanquet in his latest restatement justifies this procedure. "The state," he tells us, "is a brief expression for states *qua* states." [1] Now it may be perfectly true that there are propositions which hold of states as such, distinguishable from propositions which hold of some states and not of others ; but the urgent question for any science is how such general truths are arrived at. Is it by induction—a comparison of states, from which the points of agreement and difference may emerge ? No such inductive process is to be found in the metaphysical theory. Is it by self-evidence ? Is it, for example, self-evident " that states represent differentiations of a single human spirit . . . whose extent and intensity determine and are determined by territorial limits " ? [2] Is this a proposition which commands acceptance by intuition like a mathematical axiom ? If not, on what evidence is it based ? When Hegel asserts that the state must have a monarch to complete its personality and that the monarch must be determined by a natural method, and this is primogeniture, are these self-evident propositions ? Do they rest on intrinsic necessities revealed to Hegel's intuition or do they really do no more than clothe the practice of the Prussian state in sounding generalities ? The truth is that in social investigation large and unproven principles are apt to be either mere generalizations of customs or institutions which happen to be familiar to the writer, or expressions of his ideals, or very possibly a fusion of the two. Dr. Bosanquet thinks that his critics, dealing unguardedly " with states " (positively wandering off into the region of fact), " attribute to states that which *qua* states they are not, namely, defects which the state organization exists to remove." For him the state is the power which, as the organization

---

[1] *Social and International Ideals* (1917), p. 274. [2] Ibid., p. 275.

of the community, " has the function of maintaining the external conditions necessary to the best life." If one objects that many states maintain conditions that are quite adverse to the best life, Dr. Bosanquet retorts that we must distinguish a function from its derangement. States *qua* states do not maintain bad conditions. It results that the state is not the actual organized community, but only so much of the organized community as makes for good. This is to define the state by an ideal. But elsewhere [1] Dr. Bosanquet defines the state as that society " which is habitually recognized as a unit lawfully exercising force," a definition which would apply to the rule of the Czar or Sultan. The second definition is much nearer to common usage, which certainly thinks of the state as an organization which may serve good or bad ends, maintain good or bad conditions, but is a state as long as it holds together and maintains law and government. It is a violent departure from usage, which at best would only lead to constant misunderstanding, to restrict the term to the good elements of any such organization. But things are still worse if the state means at one time that which is actually common to stable political organizations and at another the ideal functions of a possible political organization.[2] Such methods of definition are equally fatal to science and

---

[1] *The Philosophical Theory of the State*, p. 186.

[2] It may be permissible to define a structure by its function, provided the definition be unambiguous. For this purpose the structure must only have one function, and we must know what it is, and that it is invariably performed. If every government performed the function of promoting the common good and no other, there would be no harm in defining the state as that which exists for the common good, but if, e.g., the state is in the hands of a governing class which governs for selfish ends. it does not perform this function. Do we then mean by the state the organization which sustains government or the organization which sustains a peculiar kind of government aiming at a particular kind of purpose ? If the latter, we must get another name instead of the state for every actual organization in so far as it deflects from our ideal, otherwise we shall never know whether we are talking about the ideal world or the real world.

philosophy, and our general charge against the method of idealism must be that it starts with and never corrects the fundamental confusion of the ideal and the actual.[1]

In older days we passed by the Hegelian exaltation of the state as the rhapsodical utterances of a metaphysical dreamer. It was a mistake. The whole conception is deeply interwoven with the most sinister developments in the history of Europe. It is fashionable to conceive German militarism as a product of the reaction against a beautiful sentimental idealism that reigned in the pre-Bismarckian era. Nothing could be more false. The political reaction began with Hegel, whose school has from first to last provided by far the most serious opposition to the democratic and humanitarian conceptions emanating from eighteenth-century France, sixteenth-century Holland and seventeenth-century England. It was the Hegelian conception of the state which was designed to turn the edge of the principle of freedom

[1] The truth seems to be that idealists suppose actual states to be so good that the error is insignificant. Thus, Hegel interrupts one of his rhapsodies (*Phil. des Rechts*, p. 313) with the caution, " In the idea of the state one must not have particular states before one's eyes nor particular institutions. One must rather treat the idea of this actual god on its own account (*für sich*)." For the moment the reader thinks that after all Hegel has only been romancing harmlessly about an ideal world. But he goes on, " Every state, though one may recognize this or that fault in it, has always, especially when it belongs to the developed states of our own time, the essential moments of its existence in itself." The god, it seems, is actually incarnated in actual states, though it seems to have some little trouble in the flesh.

There is a case for restricting the use of the term " state " to those political organizations which recognize the rule of law and some measure of self-government. The present writer has himself used the term in this sense (*Morals in Evolution*, ch. ii); but this still defines the state by actual and assignable features of its organization, not by the way in which that organization performs its functions ; and the term " state " is in practice used by many writers in a much wider sense, as applicable to all communities that possess an organized government. In the Hegelian state in particular, though the reign of law is certainly postulated, there is no notion of self-government.

by identifying freedom with law; of equality, by substituting the conception of discipline; of personality itself, by merging the individual in the state; of humanity, by erecting the state as the supreme and final form of human association.[1]

The direct connection between Bismarckian ethics and Hegelian teaching was ably worked out many years ago by a close student of the relations of ideas and facts in the political sphere, Mr. William Clark, but it is not in Germany alone that the Hegelian influence has profoundly affected the course of thought in one form or another. It has permeated the British world, discrediting the principles upon which liberal progress has been founded and in particular depreciating all that British and French thinkers have contributed. Perhaps it has been none the less dangerous because it has captivated men of real humanity, genuinely interested in liberal progress, so much so that in the hands of T. H. Green the Hegelian theory was for a time transmuted into a philosophy of social idealism, a variant which has a value of its own and does not lack distinguished living disciples. But as a fashionable academic philosophy genuine Hegelianism has revived, and the doctrine of the state as an incarnation of the Absolute, a super-personality which absorbs the real living personality of men and women, has in many quarters achieved the position of an academic orthodoxy. For academic purposes, indeed, it is a convenient doctrine ; its bed-rock conservatism is proof against all criticisms of the existing order. It combats the spirit of freedom in the most effective method possible, by adopting its banner and waving it from the serried battalions of a disciplined army. It justifies that negation of the individual which

---

[1] Above the state stands the Spirit which realizes itself in world history and is the absolute judge of the state. There is here a hint of a wider view which perhaps explains how it was that Karl Marx could reach internationalism from a Hegelian basis. But for Hegel combinations of states are only relative and limited (*Phil. des Rechts*, p. 314).

the modern practice of government is daily emphasizing. It sets the state above moral criticism, constitutes war a necessary incident in its existence, contemns humanity, and repudiates a Federation or League of Nations. In short, we see in it a theory admirably suited to the period of militancy and regimentation in which we find ourselves. The truth or falsity of such a theory is a matter of no small interest ; indeed, it is not a question of theory alone but of a doctrine whose historical importance is written large in the events of the nineteenth and twentieth centuries. I propose in the following lectures to set out the fundamentals of this theory and endeavour to discover the processes of thought by which, in the judgment of so many able men, the state assumes in the modern world a position which earlier ages might have given to the church or to the Deity Himself.

LECTURE II

FREEDOM AND LAW

DURING the seventeenth and eighteenth centuries established authority came under criticism from many points of view. The authority of the church was challenged by the claims of conscience; the authority of law and government was opposed by the natural right of the individual. Presently the whole social structure, the notions of political prosperity and national well-being were scrutinized in the interest of the happiness of individual men and women. It is not my purpose here to trace the movements of these theories, nor to show how in some forms they were brought round to a justification of the social order, while in others they issued in a more or less revolutionary ideal. I call attention only to the tendency to judge the state, the fabric of law and government, the structure of social institutions in terms of and by reference to the conscience or the rights or the happiness of individuals. This tendency is not very happily or fairly described when it is called a tendency to put the individual above society. This suggests a kind of ˙egoism, as though one man counted for more than millions. It is more fairly to be described as an effort to go back from institutions, laws and forms, to the real life that lay behind them, insisting that this was a life of individual men and women with souls to be saved, with personalities to be respected, or simply with capacity for feeling anguish or enjoying their brief span of life. The danger was that the emphasis on personality might be exaggerated to the point of depreciating the common life, that criticism might degenerate into anarchy, and what was valuable in the social tradition might be thrown away along with what was bad. The natural man might be endowed with none of the vices and all the virtues of his civilized counterpart, and it might be supposed that, if left to himself, or enabled to start afresh without the incubus of the established order upon him, he would build up a new life incomparably more free and beautiful. The exaggeration of revolution is the opportunity of reaction, and in the new world of theory, partly reflecting, partly anticipating the world of action, exaggerated individualism paved the way for reconstructions. Of these the most far-reaching and in the end the most influential was the metaphysical theory which challenged the whole assumption, tacit or avowed, of the critical school in all its forms, by setting up the state as a greater being, a spirit, a superpersonal entity, in which individuals with their private consciences or claims of right, their happiness or their misery, are merely subordinate elements.

The starting-point of this theory, reduced to its lowest terms, is the principle that organized society is something more than the individuals that compose it. This principle cannot be as quickly disposed of as some individualists think. Every association of men is legitimately regarded as an entity possessing certain characteristics of its own, characteristics which do not belong to the individuals apart from their membership of that association. In any human association it is true, in a sense, that the whole is something more than a sum of its parts. For example, the whole can do things which the parts severally cannot. If two men in succession push a heavy body, they may be wholly unable to move it. If they work together, they bring it along. Mechanically the summed output of energy in the two cases is equal, but in the one case it will be dissipated physically in heat, morally in the sense of frustration and loss of temper. In the other case it will succeed in its object and shift the resisting weight. The association of the two therefore has palpable effects which without the association could not be achieved. On the other hand, it is important to remark that the result of the joint effort of the two men working together is simply the sum of their efforts as they work together, though it is something other than the sum of those efforts when not co-ordinated. Any association of people involves some modification, temporary or permanent, superficial or far-reaching, in the people themselves. The work or the life of the association is something different from the work which could be achieved or the life lived by the same people apart from that association. But it does not follow that it is anything other than the sum, the expression or the result of the work that is being done, or the life that is being lived, by all the members of the association as members. When we are told, then, that the whole is more than the sum of its parts, we must reply that this depends on the sense in which the " parts " are taken. Further, we must observe that the statement, so far as it is true, is true generally ; it holds of all associations, not only of that particular association which we call the state. Family life, for example, necessarily exercises a profound influence upon its members. The family is a whole which co-operates for certain purposes and in which the various members lead lives quite other than that they would do if the family were scattered. On the other hand, the family as it stands at any given moment is simply the co-ordinated or associated whole of its members as they stand at the same moment. It is an expression of their lives so far as lived in common or in close association with one another. The family in particular has no well-being, no happiness, no good or evil fortune, which is not the well-being, the happiness, good or evil fortune of its members one or more. In an organized body, a profession, for example, a Trade Union, a business, a factory, there is again a whole numbering so many scores, hundreds, thousands of individuals as its members. In every case the members are in greater or lesser degree modified by the association into which they enter. Of the Trade Union, of the profession or business, certain things will hold true, which would not hold true of the individuals who belong to any of those associations if they did not belong to them. But again in the whole there is nothing but the co-ordinated or associated activity of the individuals which constitute it. This remains true though the organization may be permanent and the individuals changing. A college may have for hundreds of years a certain peculiar character and stamp of its own. The number of individuals passing through it and affected by it is quite indefinite. It is not constituted solely by the number present within its walls at any given time ; nor can we enumerate those who may have come within its influence during the whole period of its establishment. Nevertheless its tradition, its spirit which seems to be lodged in no single individual, is maintained by individuals, propagated from generation to generation, sometimes perhaps broken by the influx of a new type of character which fails to assimilate the tradition which it encounters.

Thus, in discussing society, we are liable to two fallacies. On the one hand we may be tempted to deny the reality of the social group, refusing to conceive it as a distinct entity, insisting on resolving it into its component individuals as though these individuals were unaffected by the fact of association. On the other side, in reaction from this exaggerated individualism, we are apt to regard society as an entity distinct from the individuals, not merely in the sense that it is an aggregate of individuals viewed in some special relation, but in the sense that it is a whole which in some way stands outside them, or in which they are merged to the prejudice of their individual identity. Further, having reached the conception of a superpersonal entity in which individuals are submerged, we are inclined to look for this entity, not in all the varied forms of associated life which intersect and cut across one another, but in some particular form of association which seems to include the rest and so to present itself as a whole to which the individual must belong as an element. This entity, idealist writers have found in the state. There are thus two points which we have to consider, first the general notion of a superpersonal entity and, secondly, the identification of this entity with the state.

We have seen that the notion of a superpersonal entity appears at first sight to express a very obvious fact. It may also appear to formulate a clear principle of ethics. The conception of duty, it may be said, teaches us that the individual lives not for himself but for a greater whole to which his own claims must be subordinated. An abstract individualism might regard the individual as possessed of certain rights, but rights are a function of the social group, since rights involve demands made upon others either for positive services or for negative forbearances. The rights of A impose obligations on B and C. They are obligations incident to and arising out of social relations, and can only be justified if their fulfilment is held to be for the good of the society—temporary or permanent—for which they are prescribed. Thus the individualistic conception defeats itself and leads us back to the whole and the duties rendered to the whole by each of its members. Now, in maintaining the superiority of the whole to any of its parts, the idealist, it may be thought, is merely asserting the superior claims of society to any one of its members. But here again there is an element of danger in the contrast between society and the individual. Any one individual is but an insignificant element in the great society, and may justly feel that his small interests must be subordinated to those of the greater body. But we cannot thus contrast a society with all the individuals which belong to it. Ethically there would be no sense in the demand for the sacrifice of all the individuals who belong or may belong to a society to the interests of that society. The million is more than the one, the interests of the million greater than the interests of the one. The question is whether the society of the million has any interests other than the conjoint interests of the million belonging to it. If the society is something other than the individuals, such a position is arguable, and we shall have to consider it as we proceed. What has to be said here is that it by no means follows from the ethical claim that the interests of the individual must give way to those of the whole to which he belongs. That claim is satisfied by the conception of the whole as the organized body of living men and women. We are not speaking here of associations that exist to promote objects beyond themselves—a conspiracy, for example, aiming at a political revolution. Here the whole society of conspirators might rightly judge that it were better for them all as individuals to perish than that the movement should be lost. " Que mon nom soit flêtri, que la France soit libre." This, indeed, might be the motto not only of the individual but of the association too. We are speaking of a society regarded as an end in itself. If we ask what good is actually realized in a society other than the good of its members, we certainly get no answer from the ethical consciousness which bids us do our duty to others and love our neighbours as ourselves. These requirements are amply recognized by the conception of ourselves as human beings placed among other human beings, whose happiness and misery our actions sensibly affect.

The method by which the idealist turns the flank of these arguments is to contend in substance that the individual possesses no independent value, ultimately we may say no independent life of his own. He is absorbed in the organized political society, the state of which he is a member. He claims freedom. The claim is admitted. Freedom is the starting-point of the Hegelian philosophy of the state, but freedom in Hegel's sense turns out to be conformity with the law and custom as interpreted by the ethical spirit of the particular society to which the individual belongs. He claims the right of judgment, he aims at a rational order of ethics. The claim is admitted but the rational order is that of the objective mind, and this on analysis turns out to be the system of institutions and customs which the state has engendered and maintains.   Finally he claims to be at least himself, an independent centre of thought and feeling, palpitating with its own emotions, subject to its own joys and sorrows, but not even selfhood is left to him, for his self is realizable only in the organized whole in which he is a kind of transitory phase.   Thus the edge of the revolutionary weapon is turned, or rather the hilt is grasped and the point directed towards the revolutionary himself.   The freedom which the revolutionary, the liberal, or for that matter the plain man of the modern world, asserts is accepted and transmuted into obedience to law.   His demand for rationality in society is granted, but granted in order to be attributed to the existing social order.   The very sense of personality, instead of being checked and chastened by the stern assertion of duty, is gently and subtly resolved into a phase or expression of the general will.   There can be no finer example of the supreme maxim of dialectical art, that the admission of an opponent's contentions is the deadliest method of refutation.

It will be convenient to set out in briefest possible terms the central points in the conception of society with which we have to deal.   The point of departure in Hegel is his doctrine of freedom.   Freedom is, in his view, falsely conceived in ordinary thought as equivalent to absence of constraint.   That is a negative and, in the end, Hegel argues, a self-contradictory idea.   True freedom is something positive.   It is self-determination. The free will is the will which determines itself.   The sense in which the will can determine itself is this, that it forms a rational whole or system of conduct, in which any particular act or deliverance of the will performs a certain necessary function.   Such a system of conduct is not achieved by the individual on his own account but is incorporated in the law and custom of society. Law alone is merely the external side of this system, but law, developed by the moral consciousness of man and worked out into the detail of custom that regulates daily life and society, constitutes the actual fabric that we require and is the objective expression of freedom. That which sustains this fabric of a rational life is the state, which is therefore the realization of the moral idea. The state is its own end, and the highest duty of the individual is to be a member of the state. Beyond the state there is no higher association and states have no duties to one another or to humanity, but their rise and fall is the process of universal history, which is the ultimate court of judgment before whose bar they come.

In order to examine this very summary account, we see we have (1) to consider the meaning of freedom. We have to understand the process of argument by which freedom is defined as self-determination and self-determination as the subordination of action to an articulate system ; (2) we have to inquire into the identification of this system with law and custom, and that will bring us (3) to the conception of the state and the reasons why it is regarded not only as an end in itself but as the supreme and the highest form of human association.

In his theory of the freedom of the will lies the key to the Hegelian theory of the state, of morality and of law. This theory consists in essentials of three positions.[1] (1) The underlying principle is that freedom consists not in the negative condition of absence of constraint but in the positive fact of self-determination. Will is freedom because it is self-determination. What then does self-determination mean ? This will bring us to the second position. The will is determined by its purposes or objects, and we are apt to think of the object as something external, pulling at it, so to say. So to think is to abandon self-determination, and in reaction from this view we think of the will as exerting free choice as between its objects. But again freedom, so conceived, is an uncharted, motiveless freedom, for if I choose one thing rather than another, there must surely

---

[1] I confine myself here to the essentials of the argument as I understand it. A somewhat expanded statement of Hegel's view will be found in Appendix I.

be something in the thing which moves me or my choice appears groundless and irrational. Here arises a form of the familiar controversy between determinism and free will which Hegel holds to be insoluble on this plane of thought. The position (2) reached then is that the will must be determined by its object, but that if this object is independent of the will, an insoluble dilemma ensues. This brings us to the third position, namely, (3) that the object of the will is determined by the will itself. Before asking how this could be, let us note the reasoning. Freedom is understood to be self-determination. The will is determined by its object, but the object is determined by the will. Ultimately, therefore, the will is self-determined and free.

But in this reasoning there appears to be a circle. How can the will be determined by its object and yet determine the object? To escape the circle we must realize that the object of the will is not outside the will at all, it is the will itself. At first sight this seems perilously near to sheer nonsense. How can the will will itself? The line of answer seems to be that the will at any given moment and in any given relation may have the whole nature of the will as its object. Thus, to suggest an example, we might think of the consistent Christian who directs his action from hour to hour by the light of a principle running right through his life. This principle he has adopted for good and all. It has become the comprehensive expression of his will. So in each act of his will it is his own will that is its object. If then the will is determined by its object, it is here determined by itself, that is, it is free.

Two lines of criticism suggest themselves. First, the Christian himself would probably say that it is not his own will but the will of God which he seeks to obey, and whatever illustration we might take, the answer would in essentials be the same. I must will something that is not yet realized, otherwise I achieve nothing. Even if I will to reform myself, the one case in which I do seem to have my own will for an object, this means that I, as I am now, set a different self before myself as something to be achieved. And if I could attain perfect consistency of action, this would mean that I should consistently serve some comprehensive end beyond myself and only to be realized by my action. The end or object then is always other than the will as it is when acting for the end. Will, like other acts of mind, has relation to an object, and things that are related are not the same. The identification of subject and object fails here as elsewhere and with it the whole scheme of self-determination breaks down.

The second criticism has a special bearing on the use which Hegel makes of his definition of freedom. Grant, for the sake of argument, that self-determination is something more than absence of constraint. But it is not less than absence of constraint. Where and in so far as an act of will is constrained, it is not free. What is absolutely free is absolutely unconstrained. What is relatively free is relatively unconstrained. Freedom in one thing may indeed imply restraint on something else —if I am secure in freedom to go about my business, this implies that others are prevented from hindering me in doing so—but the thing which is free is not in the respect in which it is free also restrained. To be free in one part or in one relation it will have to be restrained in another part or relation, but in that in which it is restrained it is not also free.

Now in adopting a principle of conduct we may be acting on our own motion in response to an internal conviction. So far we are free. But the principle may be such as to put heavy constraint on a part of our nature, and if so, that part of our nature is not free. We may be slaves to our principles, as well as to our impulses, and in fact common experience tells us that there are those who would be better men without their principles, if they would only give their natural emotions free play. But a life of uncharted impulses cannot be free, because unregulated impulses not only restrain but utterly frustrate and destroy one another. But neither is a life of narrow principle free, because such a principle at best holds a great part of us subdued, perhaps sullen and unsatisfied.[1] In a word freedom for one element in our nature, be it an impulse or a conviction, may mean the subjection of the rest of our nature. If there be such a thing as freedom for our personality as a whole, its parts must have as much scope as is compatible with their union. This cannot mean absolute freedom for each part, for no one must override the remainder. It means freedom limited by the conditions of development in harmony, and by nothing else. If we suppose a whole of many parts capable of a harmonious development, and if we suppose this whole to be subject to no restraints except those which it itself imposes on its parts to secure the common development, then we have an intelligible sense in which the whole may be termed free. Now the self is a whole capable of a harmonious development, and it may be termed free when it orders its life accordingly. The principle of freedom then springs from the nature of the self as a coherent whole. It is to be distinguished from a principle cramping harmony of development, even if accepted by our own consent. Still more is it to be distinguished from one imposed from without by suggestion, authority and perhaps some mingling of compulsion. Now Hegel does not draw these distinctions. Discarding absence of constraint from the idea of freedom, and concentrating attention on the element of unity which the will undoubtedly introduces into action, he tends to identify freedom with mere acceptance of a principle of conduct and thus paves the way for its further identification with law. He saw that freedom involved restraint on something but did not see that it was restraint on something else, that which is free being in the respect in which it is free necessarily unconstrained.

---

[1] It may be said that it is the function of will to subdue nature, but this is precisely to give it the freedom of a despot, and leave the personality unfree. To do Hegel justice, no such antithesis seems contemplated in his argument.

Hegel's first position is now before us. Freedom for him rests not on absence of constraint but on the acceptance of a principle expressing the true nature of rational will running through and unifying all the diverse purposes of men. The embodiment of such a principle and therefore of freedom Hegel finds in the system of right and law. Two terms here require some consideration before the meaning of this principle can be understood. By the term "embodiment" I have rendered the word *Daseyn*. *Daseyn* in the Hegelian philosophy is a term used in contradistinction to what we ordinarily call a mere idea or bare thought of a thing, for example, or to its mere potentiality. We must not, however, translate the word *Daseyn* by "reality" or even by "existence," as both of these terms are assigned to distinct phases in the Hegelian dialectical development. We may, however, think of the embodiment of a political idea in an Act of Parliament or of a political principle in an institution or a constitution, as giving what Hegel would call *Daseyn* to that idea or that principle. That being understood, we see in general the meaning of the phrase that freedom is embodied in right. But the term "right" or law also requires comment. Hegel's term is *Recht*, and it would seem better to use the German term whenever ambiguity is to be feared. According to Dr. Bosanquet it is the advantage of the German term that it maintains in itself the intimate relation between right and law. It may be urged on the contrary that the very fact that German writers use one term for these two related but quite distinct notions is an obstacle to clear thinking in their Jurisprudence and Ethics in general, and in the Hegelian philosophy in particular. The consequence of its use is that we begin and go on with the confusion of two issues, which it is the particular purpose of social philosophy to hold distinct. The one issue is the nature of right, the foundation of moral obligation, the meaning, value and authority of a moral system ; and the other the meaning, value and authority of law; and the final question of political philosophy consists of the relation between these two distinct things. That relation can never be clearly set forth if we use terms which imply a confusion between the terms related.

But in what sense is *Recht* the embodiment of freedom ? Let us first, for the sake of accuracy, supply a correction, without which we should do injustice to Hegel, though the correction does not touch the essence of the question. Mere law is only an external embodiment of freedom, Hegel fully admits. Law is abstract, general, and regards primarily the externals of behaviour ; to complete it we want something which is on the one hand more concrete, more closely adapted to the requirements of individual life, and, on the other hand, something expressing the inner acceptance of the rule of society as well as its external observance. This conception we find in the word *Sittlichkeit*, a term which can hardly be rendered in English by a single word. We cannot translate it " morality," because Hegel uses the word *Moralität* as something which is purely inward and subjective, whereas *Sittlichkeit* is objective as well. Dr. Bosanquet translates it by the phrase " ethical use and wont," and we may understand it as the whole system of customs and traditions as accepted by the normal member of a society, as forming the fabric within which he has to live. This system is, in Hegel's phrase, the conception of freedom come to self-consciousness in the world in which we live.[1] Restating our question therefore we have to ask, in what sense is the social tradition an embodiment of freedom ? The examination of this question takes us into the heart of the Hegelian conception of the relation of the individual man to society, and this again will be found to be a particular case of the relation of the individual to the universal, which is the central point of the Hegelian metaphysics.

It will have been noticed in discussing the Hegelian theory of the will we have always to speak of *the* will. We have not spoken of the wills of different men and

[1] *Phil. des Rechts*, p. 205.

their relations to one another. We have never used the plural term. We have always spoken of the will as though it were one substantive reality ; and this is in fact the Hegelian view. But in society there are many wills and in obedience to law we conform, as we suppose, to the will of another. How then can we talk of *the* will as if there were only one ? The question will lead us ultimately into the metaphysical problem of the one and the many, for the Hegelian theory of the universal underlies the whole issue. But let us first set out the problem with more fullness and consider the solution proffered by Hegel's most recent and most faithful exponent.

At the first blush it must be owned it is difficult to attach any clear meaning to the statement that the social tradition is the actual or concrete realization of freedom. Freedom, as we have been told, means self-determination. Self-determination, we were further told, implies determination by a principle as against mere impulse. But even if we waive for the moment all controversies on these points, it remains that if there is self-determination, the determining principle must be a principle of our own choosing, an expression of our own character, the real bent of our own selves. The established ethical tradition may of course fall in with our desires, and if so, we are aware of no constraint in accepting it, but socially and ethically the question of freedom only arises where there is a clash of wills. Suppose then that our will happens to be in conflict at one point with the social tradition, what are we to understand ? To say that in such a case we ought to yield up our judgment and conform is at least an intelligible, though sometimes a disputable proposition ; but that is not what is said or intended. The proposition before us is that in conforming to the social tradition and only in conforming to it we are free. It does not appear to matter whether we ourselves find the rule which it propounds contrary to our happiness or opposed to our conscience. Our freedom lies it would seem, in the surrender of our own happiness, even in the stifling of our own conscience, for we are free only as we conform to the moral tradition embodied in and supported by the state. Freedom is self-determination, yet freedom is realized only in the submission of self to something which may at any time conflict with all that is strongest and all that is deepest in ourselves. The use and wont of the organized political society to which we belong may, for example, at certain points conflict with the teaching of the religious body to which we belong, or it may involve injustices and oppressions against which our conscience comes to revolt. Now it is not merely contended that in such a conflict we ought to surrender our judgment. That is at least arguable. It is contended that in submitting ourselves, and in this alone, we are actually free. We seem faced with something like a contradiction. And, however we define the state, this particular contradiction does not seem to be resolved. For we may think of it as essentially an organization of persons like ourselves. In that case, in obeying it against our own will we are simply under the constraint of others ; or we may think of it as something impersonal, superpersonal, or, as Hegel calls it, divine, and in that case we are obeying an impersonal or divine authority. Even if we are free in yielding to it, that would seem to be the last act of our freedom. It is an abdication, a final discharge of our authority over ourselves.

Now something like this conception of the relation of freedom to the general will goes back to Rousseau. Dr. Bosanquet [1] quotes Rousseau as saying " that whoever shall refuse to obey the general will shall be constrained to do so by the whole body, which means nothing else than that he will be forced to be free." He goes on to say, " In this passage Rousseau lays bare the very heart of what some would call political faith and others political superstition. This lies in the conviction that the ' moral person which constitutes the state ' is a reality." If we follow the development of this con-

[1] *The Philosophical Theory of the State*, pp. 95, 96.

ception, we shall find the key to the difficulty before us. Reviewing his examination of Rousseau, the details of which we need not follow, Dr. Bosanquet writes : " (a) The negative relation of the self to other selves begins to dissolve away before the conception of the common self and (b) the negative relation of the self to law and government begins to disappear in the idea of a law which expresses our real will as opposed to our trivial and rebellious moods. The whole notion of man as one among others tends to break down and we begin to see something in the one which actually identifies him with the others and at the same time tends to make him what he admits he ought to be." This passage really seems to contain the sum and substance of Idealistic Social Philosophy. There is a common self, and this is no metaphor. It does not mean a community among selves because " the whole notion of man as one among many tends to break down." It is a self which is a higher unity than the legal or moral person, and this self seems to be identified with the real will, which is also, it seems, the self that one ought to be.

We now begin to see why that which appears to us a stark contradiction is seen in quite a different light by the idealist. Our difficulty was that self-determination cannot be the same thing as determination by other selves, or by an impersonal state. The answer is that the division between self and others dissolves away into the conception of a common self and the division between the individual and the state disappears in the conception of a law expressing our own real will ; so that in conforming to law, we are submitting ourselves neither to other persons nor to something impersonal. We are conforming to our own real will. But if in point of fact we happen to will just the opposite to that which the law ordains, how can this be ? The answer lies in the distinction between the actual and the real will. We must give Dr. Bosanquet's statement of this distinction with some fullness.

" It was observed above that what Rousseau had before him in his notion of the General Will might be described as the ' Will in itself,' or the Real Will. Any such conception involves a contrast between the Real Will and the Actual Will, which may seem to be meaningless. How can there be a Will which is no one's Will ? and how can anything be my Will which I am not fully aware of, or which I am even averse to ? This question will be treated more fully on psychological grounds in a later chapter. For the present, it is enough to call attention to the plain fact that often when people do not know what they mean, they yet mean something of very great importance ; or that, as has commonly been said, ' what people demand is seldom what would satisfy them if they got it.' We may recall the instances in which even Mill admitted that it is legitimate to infer, from the inherent nature of the will, that people do not really ' will ' something which they desire to do at a given moment. . . . Now the contradiction, which here appears in an ultimate form, pervades the actual ' will, which we exert from moment to moment as conscious individuals, through and through. A comparison of our acts of will through a month or a year is enough to show that no one object of action, as we conceive it when acting, exhausts all that our will demands. Even the life which we wish to live, and which on the average we do live, is never before us as a whole in the motive of any particular volition. In order to obtain a full statement of what we will, what we want at any moment must at least be corrected and amended by what we want at all other moments ; and this cannot be done without also correcting and amending it so as to harmonize it with what others want, which involves an application of the same process to them. But when any considerable degree of such correction.and amendment had been gone through, our own will would return to us in a shape in which we should not know it again, although every detail would be a necessary inference from the whole of wishes and resolutions which we actually cherish. And if it were to be supplemented and readjusted so as to stand not merely for the life which on the whole we manage to live, but for a life ideally without contradiction, it would appear to us quite remote from anything which we know."

Postponing for a moment any critical examination of this conception, let us take stock of our position. According to Dr. Bosanquet, then, there is underlying the actual will, of which we are aware, a deeper real will, which is the actual will reorganized and made completely consistent or coherent. It is in fact that organized system of purposes which we found in the

Hegelian will, and in a later passage Dr. Bosanquet adopts the Hegelian phrase—" the will that wills itself."

But now, if we grant for the moment this underlying will and suppose ourselves to be free only when we conform to it, we still have not reached the connection between the real self and the common self, which is the state, in which the distinction between self and others is absorbed and whose will is expressed in the social tradition. The connection is explained by Dr. Bosanquet (p. 123), where we are told, " The habits and institutions of any community are, so to speak, the standing interpretation of all the private wills which compose it." And this seems to be taken as the content both of the general and the real will. It is an imperfect representation of the real will because " every set of institutions is an incomplete embodiment of life." On the other hand " the complex of social institutions " is " very much more complete than the explicit ideas which at any given instant move any individual mind in volition."

The essence of the position is now before us. Moral freedom—we shall see later that Dr. Bosanquet candidly recognizes the distinction between moral and legal liberty —lies in conformity to the real will. The real will is the general will and is expressed in the social fabric. The expression is not perfect and admits of progressive development, but it is in the main what we require. Social tradition, if not the complete expression of ourselves, is the fullest available to us at any given time. The vehicle of social tradition, or rather the organizing principle which gives it vitality, meaning and coherence, is the state. The state, therefore, is the true self in which the mere individual is absorbed. This is the corner stone of moral and political obligation. Briefly, we are morally free when our actions conform to our real will, our real will is the general will, and the general will is most fully embodied in the state. These are the governing positions of the metaphysical theory which we have to examine.

LECTURE III

THE REAL WILL

(a) THE steps by which the conception of the real will is reached by Dr. Bosanquet are contained in the passage quoted in the last lecture, and may be summarized thus. What we will from moment to moment is called our actual will. This actual will is always incomplete and often contradictory and inharmonious. To get at a full statement of what we will it would have to be corrected by (a) what we want at all other moments, and (b) by what others want. If this correction were carried far enough, our " own will would return to us in a shape in which we should not know it again." Yet the whole process would only have been a logical series of inferences from the whole of the wishes and resolutions which we actually cherish. And if, going further than this, we suppose criticism carried to a point at which it would achieve a life ideally without contradiction, then the will to such a life " would appear to us quite remote from anything which we know." Remote as it is, this is what Dr. Bosanquet seems to mean by the real will. We are then left with the paradox that our real will may be something which we never really will because we do not even know it and could not recognize it if it were set before us.

What is the explanation of this paradox? How does Bosanquet arrive at it? (1) The justification appears to be that the objects which we set before us, at which we consciously aim, are not always what we really want. They do not really satisfy us. This is a form of words expressing of course a perfectly well-known truth. A man's nature is constantly driving him on to ends which he imperfectly appreciates and the concrete shapes which these ends take are often quite unsatisfactory. They give illusions of desirability which cheat him on attaining them. None the less, so far as he really chooses them that choice is for the time being his real will, in the true sense of real as that which is not merely supposed to be but is. Moreover, the fact that he so chooses them and makes a mistake in doing so is a real limitation of his will. The illusoriness of the will is precisely as hard a fact, as stubborn a reality, as the persistent background of want and unrest, which is the other side of the matter. The man's will is in short just what it is with all its limitations and not what it might be if these limitations were removed. It may be suggested, and this is what Bosanquet seems to mean, that logically a man must be taken to will all that his actual will implies. But this is quite fallacious. On the contrary, show me a consequence following from an act of my will, which I have not yet seen, and it is quite possible that I may recoil from it. In any case the act seen with fresh implications is a different act, the will which chooses it a different will. We may reasonably say that the man who has gone through the long process of criticism and judgment described by Bosanquet in the evolution of the real will has become in that process a very different man.

But there is a more fundamental objection to the term "real will." Strictly there is no part in me which is more real than any other part. There are elements in me which are more permanent, and if the self is permanent, there are, let us say, moods or actions which really belong to myself more than others do, but one mood is not more real a mood or one act more real an act than another. The term "Real" is in fact in such passages as these used rhetorically, that is, in a way which does not distinguish between its adjectival meaning, connecting a particular phase of myself with myself as a whole, and its substantival meaning, in which the term " Reality " is something which must either be simply asserted or simply denied, and there is no more or less. A particular emotion is either something which I have and then it is real, whether permanent or transitory, reasonable or unreasonable ; or it is something which, say, you falsely attribute to me and then it is unreal. For the contrast between the real and the unreal then should be substituted the contrast between the self as it is permanently constituted and the self as it acts in some transitory excitement.

(2) The real will then, if it means anything, means the permanent underlying nature of any one of us, but this again does not mean our nature as it might be if we were spiritually born again, transformed by no matter what process of rational reflection, hortatory suggestion or moral and emotional re-orientation. This has a most important bearing on our second position. Dr. Bosanquet's assumption is that the real will is in fact identical with the general will. The supposed ground is that the real will must be one which would be perfectly harmonious with itself. This is assumed to involve a harmony with other wills. The assumption begs the principal question of Ethics, but let it pass for the moment. Let us agree that the perfectly rationalized will involves a harmony of self and others. What ground is there for assuming that this harmony would express the true permanent nature of John Jones ? John Jones, if you unrolled before him the life which you expected him to lead as a rational being, might repel it with scorn. He might say, if articulate enough, that it makes no room for certain elements which he finds very real in him, his passions, his physical appetites, his desires to get the better of others. How are you to prove to him that these are not real parts of himself ? The answer seems to be that if you carry John Jones through the process of rational criticism, he will discover elements of contradiction in these warring desires. As long as you present this to him as an intellectual proposition, how-

ever, John Jones will reply, " Consistency be hanged !
I will have my life in parts, each as good as I can make
it. It is these that are the true John Jones." To this
again the only reply available seems to be that the process
of revealing the true rational harmony to John Jones
cannot be an intellectual process merely, it must be one
which touches his emotions, his will itself. But what
is this but to admit that the true John Jones must
undergo a change ? If he is to be formed into a rational
will, he must be transformed. I would be far from
denying that every human being is capable of such reformation. I insist only that it is a reformation which is
a transformation and that the will, which Bosanquet
calls real and which I would call rational, harmonious
or simply good, is not real in the average man, nor even
in its completeness in the best of men.[1] Bosanquet's

---

[1] In the discussion of the criminal (pp. 226, etc.) there are some
instructive remarks, illustrating the nature of the real will.
Bosanquet says justly that if an uneducated man were told that
" in being punished for an assault he was realizing his own will,
he would think it cruel nonsense." Some who are not the criminal
might also think it nonsense ; and the only reason why they should
not think it assigned by Bosanquet is (*a*) that the criminal would
quite well understand that he was being served, as he would say,
in the same way as somebody else would be served who had done
the same thing. (*b*) That the punishment is the reaction on the
criminal of a system of rights to which he is a party. As to (*a*)
the essential difference between the criminal and the good will
is that while the criminal may be prepared to judge others, he
makes exceptions in favour of himself. Very often he cannot
see the identity of his act with another which he condemns and
even if he can see it, so far as he is criminal, his attitude is " I
don't care." If an acute dialectician were to argue with him,
he would no doubt entangle him in inconsistencies and show that
if he were a reasonable man, and if he admitted universal rules
applying to himself and others, he would not be a criminal. But
if this argument is to have effect, it must not only convince the
man's intelligence but convert his will. In order genuinely to
condemn himself, the criminal must therefore become another
man than that which he in fact is. And we see very clearly from
this instance that the good, rational or social will imputed to the
criminal as his real will is precisely the will that the criminal, as
criminal, really does not possess. The fallacy consists in describ-

own description of course shows he is perfectly aware of this, yet he confuses the whole issue by the use of the adjective "real." It is misleading to contrast real with transitory, trivial aims. It is not merely one's superficial or casual interests that clash with others and exhibit contradiction with one another so that they interfere with the best life, it is also the deepest passions and sometimes the most fervid conscience. A man may feel, and the feeling may be no illusion, that a personal passion goes to the very foundation of his being, and yet the passion may be lawless or it may collide with the entire bent of his life in other directions, his devotion to public duty, for example, or perhaps deeprooted obligations of family and friendship. If the real self means that which goes deep, we cannot deny that it contains possibilities of contradiction far more serious than the collision between permanent interest and passing desire.

There is conceivable a will which is perfectly rational and harmonious in all its deliverances. There is conceivable a system of wills so harmonizing with themselves

ing as a real will something which a logician regards as being implied in the actual will of the criminal. This implication rests on some principle of impartiality which the logician may have very good grounds for maintaining ; but this is precisely the principle which the criminal, as criminal, either ignores or definitely rejects. As to (*b*), at bottom the same analysis applies. The criminal acquiesces in the system as far as he chooses, as far as he finds it suits him, or perhaps as far as he is unable to resist it, but, *qua* criminal, does not in the least care for the inconsistency, as a rational man would judge it to be, involved in his departure from the system where that departure suits him better. In brief, the murderer does not really want himself to be hanged unless he has repented and ceased to be the man that he was when he committed the murder.

It must be added here that the conception of punishment as expressing the will of the offender has a sinister application to the rebel. It may be said that the rebel has accepted the social system and thereby the punishment which will follow upon him when he comes to challenge it. From the rebel's point of view the answer may be that he never willingly accepted the social system as a whole but found himself involved in it and could not react against it until the moment for rebellion had arrived.

and with one another ; such a perfect harmony we may legitimately speak of as the ideally rational life and the ideally good life and, as such, may contrast it with any actual life which is imperfect in these respects. Again, we may grant that there is something real within us which answers to the conception of such a life, and something real within any society of human beings which, in a sense, moves us towards such a life. At any rate, from the nature of the case contradiction tends to defeat itself and harmony to fructify. Thus by continual trial and error society moves on. Unfortunately the inharmonious elements are equally real and the disharmonies are not merely trivial, transitory, superficial, but rooted in the structure of the self and, what is almost as important, in the social structure. Every group of human beings acquires a corporate life and with it only too probably a collective selfishness, which over long periods may hold the development of other groups in arrest. The contrast is between the rational harmonious good and the irrational conflicting bad. When this contrast is confused with the contrast between the real and the unreal the problem is stated in wrong terms and does not admit of solution. The peculiar vice of this statement is that, in laying down a certain kind of life as expressing the real will of the individual, the ground is prepared for the argument that in the compulsion of the individual to lead such a life there is no interference with his real will. He is supposed to be merely unable to judge for himself. Thus, in principle, there is no limitation to restraints upon the individual, no core of freedom which collective action should not touch. And yet it must be plain that no actual human being, or association of human beings, knows what the real will is, for it is admitted that the process of eliciting it is so roundabout and involved that a man would not recognize his real will if it was put before him. Why not then admit that it is not real but ideal— an ideal which is beyond human nature though it may be a legitimate object of human endeavour ?

(*b*) **The General Will.** If for the " real " we write the

4

ideal or rational will, we have next to ask whether this would be a general will. We may grant that if the will in you or me were made completely rational, it would accept principles upon which we should agree. Thus, in all rational wills there would be a qualitative identity. We should so far be like one another in our fundamental attitude towards life and conduct. But when we pass from the conception of like persons or like selves to a corporate person or a common self, there is an inevitable transition from qualitative sameness to the sameness of continuity and numerical unity. The assumptions are (1) There is in me a real self, my real will, which is opposed to what I very often am. (2) This real will is what I ought to be as opposed to what I very often am. (3) There is in you a real will and in every other member of society a real will. All these real wills are what you and every other member of society ought to be. In quality and character these real wills are indistinguishable. They are therefore the same. (4) This sameness constitutes of all the real wills together one self. But the kind of unity involved in what is called qualitative identity or sameness of character is quite a different unity from that involved in the self or from that involved in the state. The self is a continuous identity united by strands of private memory and expectation, comprising elements of feeling, emotion and bodily sensation, which are its absolute exclusive property. No such continuity unites distinct selves, however alike, or however united in their objects. So at least it seems to those whom Dr. Bosanquet dismisses with contempt as " theorists of the first look." For them human individuality is and remains something ultimate. To Dr. Bosanquet on the other hand [1] individuality is only a particular case of the distinct contribution offered by parts within a system which he calls the universal. The differences within the self are for him in their essential nature identical with the differences between selves. I am of course in a sense one, but I am in a sense many. I am a centre of many experiences,

[1] *The Philosophical Theory of the State*, ch. vii.

and even of many groups of experiences, each of which has its own controlling principle. This makes me, as popular metaphor has always recognized, a kind of miniature state ; and for Bosanquet this metaphor expresses the real truth. Two passages may be taken as summing up his discussion.

" If we consider my unity with myself at different times as the limiting case, we shall find it very hard to establish a difference between the unity of what we call one ' mind ' and that of all the ' minds ' which enter into a single social experience." [1]

And again in the following chapter : [2]

" Individuals are limited and isolated in many ways, but their true individuality does not lie in their isolation but in that distinctive act or service by which they pass into unique contributions to the universal."

Common sense confronted by these statements has a feeling of outrage which makes it disinclined to argue. It is inclined to say that the difference between self and another is as plain as the difference between black and white, and that if a man does not see it, there is nothing plainer to appeal to. It is inclined to add that, if certain views of the state are reduced to justifying themselves by such confusion as this, that is their sufficient refutation.

But it is not quite satisfactory to leave the argument at this point. We must trace the roots of the fallacy. Let us first ask in what sense it is true that individuals have a common life or a common experience. To begin with they live in the same world. A and B may be said to have a common experience when they both perceive the same object. For example, both are reading the same book, studying the same subject, have before their eyes the same rose, are partners in one enterprise, members of one society. Here is a real unity, a numerical unity, but this unity is in the outer world, the world with which both minds are in contact. It may be in the actual existing world, as in the case of the rose which

[1] P. 178.   [2] P. 183.

both see and both smell, or it may be in the processes of the world and the changes to which both contribute, the purpose which both desire to realize, but in any case it is external to both. The unity is in the object—a term here which may be conveniently used in its popular ambiguity as meaning sometimes a real thing, sometimes a purpose. The individuals are subjects, distinct centres of sensation, perception, thought, feeling, active will, standing in relation to that object. They are two, while the object is one. But, secondly, even between A and B, as two, there is a kind of unity. They are, or may be, similarly affected by or to the object. The rose smells sweet to both. The success of the business is an object of eager interest to both. The relation here is one which some would call resemblance, others identity of character. When spoken of as identity of character it is easily merged in thought with the numerical identity belonging to the object. Nevertheless it is a distinct relation. These then are the two foundations of identity as between individuals, the relationship to an identical world and the partial identity of character in themselves.

How do these relations differ fundamentally from the relations between parts of my experience to one another? For example, I may smell the same rose twice and pursue the same object through successive days and with considerable differences of mood, slackening and tensioning of interest and so on. The answer is that there is something common in me to all my acts and experiences which is never common to you and me. I am aware in myself not only of the object that I experience but of the act of experiencing it, but I am never aware of your act of experiencing any object. Certainly I believe that you experience objects but I believe it on inference, you being a person like myself and acting in ways sufficiently similar to mine to enable me to interpret them. When it is said that our experience is common there is an ambiguity in the term "experience" which is overlooked. There is a sense in which you share my experience. There is also a sense in which your experience is absolutely and for ever private to you, and mine absolutely and for ever private to me. Experience may mean a series of objects that is before the mind, and in that sense it may be common, or it may mean what Professor Alexander calls enjoyment, or what might with more propriety be called suffering. Mind is always dealing with objects, apprehending them, thinking about them, operating upon them and so on. The dealing, the thinking is not the object dealt with, the object thought about, it is the act or state that is enjoyed or suffered. True it becomes known and is in that sense an object, but it is an object of a distinct class, the character of which class is that everything in it is known as the subject of some other object. The entire system of these subjective acts or states forms a continuum, constituting what I know within me as my individuality or myself. My consciousness of myself rests upon a distinction between this thread of enjoyment and suffering and the entire system of the objects to which it relates, and my sense of personal identity is my recognition of the continuity of this thread. This is the element of isolation which, in contradiction to Bosanquet's dictum, is the true core of individuality. This isolation is not merely physical. My body is a part of the objective world to me. I know it by the senses as I know the rose, but the experience, as suffering, is always located in the body, felt within the body, and the physical separateness of my body from another, though not the ground of my isolation, is inseparably connected with it. What in practical philosophy is even more important is that the whole series of my feelings belongs to the thread of suffering. True, I am aware of my feelings and can name and classify them and to that extent they are objects to me, but I always know them as feelings of my own, which I enjoy or suffer as being attributes or states of the subjective continuum that is distinct from the outer world as being in me incommunicably private. When I am said to share another's feeling, that is confused metaphor. The sight of another's pain may arouse pain in me but it is another pain.

Normally, it is not even qualitatively the same pain. I do not feel toothache when my child is suffering from toothache but pity or anxiety, an emotion not a sensation. There are cases of what is sometimes conceived to be sympathy in the strictest sense in which the sight or description of physical torture seems to stimulate something of the same anguish in myself, but even here it is a qualitative and not a numerical identity that is in question. And it is fortunate that it is so, for if I felt all the real anguish of the sufferer, I should hardly be in a position to come to his relief.

We trace the foundations of Dr. Bosanquet's identification of individuals then to a confusion in the use of the term "experience." Experience as meaning a world of objects may be common to many selves. Experience as that which each self enjoys or suffers is absolutely private. In the former sense different minds can enter into a single experience ; in the latter sense never, though they may know about one another's experience. In the former sense experience is not as such a universal but rather one comprehensive world of objects to which all individuals are related. In the latter sense it is a universal in the true sense of a class of individual beings resembling one another or possessing identities of character.[1]

---

[1] It would be unfair to Dr. Bosanquet to suggest that he ignores the exclusiveness of consciousness. In the present work he tells us, for example (p. 183), " In a sense it is true that no one consciousness can partake of or can actually enter into another." And similarly in his *Principle of Individuality and Value* he writes (p. 47) : " No one would attempt to overthrow what we have called the formal distinctness of selves or self. This consists in the impossibility that one finite centre of experience should possess as its own immediate experience the immediate experience of another." But he seems to regard what we have called enjoyment as a kind of form, to which the object of experience gives content. So in the same work a little earlier (p. 38) we read : " The pure privacy and incommunicability of feeling as such is superseded in all possible degrees by the self-transcendence and universality of the contents with which it is unified ; and as these contents are constituents of our individuality, the conception that

The privacy of enjoyed experience, and in particular of feeling, has an important bearing on the doctrine of force

individuality or personality has its centre in the exclusiveness of feeling, neglects the essential feature of individuality or personality itself. It has an aspect of distinct unshareable immediacy ; but in substance and stuff and content, it is universal, communicable, expansive." And so we learn a little later (p. 48) that the inevitable distinctness of any immediate experience, which is said to contain the essence of individuality, is a very different thing from the inexplicable and fundamental foreignness commonly postulated as between different persons. " It merely comes to this, that they are organizations of content, which a difference of quality, generally though not strictly dependent on belonging to different bodies, prevents from being wholly blended." There must, it would seem, be some characteristic differences between you and me, just as there are characteristic differences between any two parts of the same thing, but not such as to interfere with our fundamental sameness, not radically distinct from the differences which may be discerned within myself at different times or in different relations. This position is developed on p. 58. " With the one exception, of the thread of cœnæsthesia, compatible with any degree of hostility and foreignness, there is no ground of unity with our past and future selves which would not equally carry us to unity and fellowship with others and with the world. Our certainty of their existence is in both cases inferential, and on the same line of inference, both are cemented to it by the same stuff and material of unity, language, ideas, purposes, contents of communicable feeling ; and, as we have seen, the other may in these ways be far more closely knit with me than is my previous self." Hence we are not surprised to learn in the same book (p. 62) that " Separateness is not an ultimate character of the individual, but is a phase of being akin to externality, and tending to disappear in so far as true individuality prevails." It appears from these passages that in spite of admissions as to the exclusiveness of finite centres of experience, the radical distinction between the subject and the object, between enjoyment and things experienced, escapes Dr. Bosanquet. His whole world is, as it were, on one plane. It is all experience more or less articulate and complete, more or less partial and confused. Individuality means a relatively high level of articulateness, and for that reason all individualities, in proportion as they develop, approximate to one and the same limit, the single experience which is wholly articulate. This conception of the entire fabric leading up to it and down from it falls to the ground as soon as subject and object are distinguished.

and freedom. When Bosanquet comes in chapter viii to deal with the limits of state action he finds the difficulty to lie in the antithesis between force and the spiritual character of the real will. The state has to rely on rewards and punishments (p. 190) that destroy the value of an action " as an element in the best life." " An action performed in this sense under compulsion is not a true part of the will." This, so far as it goes, is very sound and undoubtedly touches one of the true motives for restricting the operations of the state,[1] but

---

[1] It is only fair to Dr. Bosanquet to say that he recognizes the character of moral liberty more fully than some other writers and in particular than Hegel. His general conception of liberty, as explained in *The Philosophical Theory of the State*, is that the self is free when it is master of its passions, or, more precisely, when the real will is the master of the false will. But it is recognized by a piece of candour, which should be acknowledged, that this is not the literal or elementary sense of liberty. That literal sense means the absence of constraint exercised by one upon others, and in going beyond that we are more or less making use of a metaphor (p. 137). It is, however, maintained that we may acquiesce as " rational beings in a law and order, which on the whole makes for the possibility of asserting our true or universal selves, at the very moment when this law and order is constraining our particular private wills in a way which we resent or even condemn." The term " condemn " here is odd. Does it mean we condemn the law judicially, that is rationally ? If so, there would seem to be a contradiction. What Bosanquet must mean is that we recognize law to be necessary, or rather perhaps recognize law-abidingness to be necessary even if a particular law is bad. But the real question lies beyond this. In what sense is law as such an instrument of moral liberty ? The suggestion is apparently that the coercive repression of warring impulses in me sets my real, that is rational, will free. Thus, there would be no objection in theory to the plan of making men good by legislation. But this hardly seems to express Bosanquet's own meaning because at a later stage he frankly recognizes the limits of coercion, and fundamentally the whole idea is untrue. If my rational will has conquered the erring impulse, then it has established its own mastery, and may be called free in the moral sense. But, if and in so far as the erring impulse is overcome by an external restraint, my will is not only not free but not even effective. The best that can be said for making men good by coercion is that coercive restraints at a given moment may prevent an irreparable error

the denial of individuality leads Bosanquet to repudiate
the view that force, or generally speaking state interference, lies in the intrusion of others upon the self (see
p. 183). To him in principle there are no others. I
should be inclined to subjoin that, if that is so, there is
no force. What is at the back of force and what does it
rest upon? The isolation of the individual. When we
speak of forcing a man to do a certain kind of action,
we do not mean that we take hold of his hands and make
him do it. A nurse may do that with a small child but
it is not what is intended or practical in adult life. What
we mean is that pains and penalties are imposed, that
there is an appeal to fear of future suffering or to the
hope of future reward. Now when A puts forth force
on B, what is the situation? B, let us suppose, is the
subject of a certain impulse, craving or feeling which is
absolutely private to him, not shared and not necessarily
in the least understood by A. B, if he yields to this
impulse, is under the fiat of A to suffer a penalty. Once
more the feeling of pain, grief, perhaps agony, is absolutely private to him, unshared and perhaps little
appreciated by A. The danger is that A may be indifferent
to B's feelings. There is nothing necessarily to com-
municate to A the experience either of the craving or of
the penalty by which he represses it. Now if A literally
shared all B's experiences, there would not be this danger.
In prescribing for B, A would have to go through the same
thing himself and would have to take his own prescription.
If there were always this community of experience in
the sense of a community of suffering, there would be no
special practical danger in the use of force, and in a
democratic and uniform society we do in fact expect
to find greater mildness in the use of penalties to which
all are equally exposed. But in so far as there is a dis-

and so make it possible for me to recover my genuine self-control
later on ; just as, if I am prevented from suicide, I have at least
the opportunity of living to do better another day. But if I am
permanently in tutelage, I am permanently unfree and without
means of freedom.

tinction between the governors and the governed, the use of force is subject to great abuse, which consists precisely in the fact that it is an intrusion on one set of people by others who are in a large measure immune from the practical working consequences.

We may carry the theoretical point a little further, and we may ask if a man could ever put force upon himself in the sense in which he could put force upon another. We have seen that when he puts force upon another there is the threat of pain, not necessarily following from the action and not a pain which he will feel himself. Neither of these conditions is realized when a man puts force on himself. When a man puts force upon himself he conquers an impulse, that is to say, he brings the whole force of his nature to bear, or more accurately, the organized system of convictions, principles, interests, which is his personality, and does not in truth so much conquer himself as win a victory for himself. He does not threaten himself with a penalty which he will not share. He does not, strictly speaking, threaten himself at all. It is true he may fear a penalty, remorse it may be, or a headache it may be, and he may say to himself that this will follow as surely as day follows night. This, however, is not a threat but an anticipation, and it is an anticipation, not of something arbitrarily attached *ab extra* to the act, but of something following from it as an inherent consequence. Obviously, too, it is not something from which the author of the supposed menace is to be immune. The only sense in which a man can be said to threaten himself would be under some artificial form of self-reformation in which a man undertakes a vow to himself to undergo a specific penance for a specific trespass. Such a case, if we may regard it as real, would be an analogical transfer to the sphere of self of the relation of self and others, and can only belong to the sphere of play-acting with our moral nature.

I conclude, therefore, that the use of force is essentially what Bosanquet denies it to be. It is an imposition on the individual by others, and its practical dangers lie precisely in that isolation of the individual feelings through which force acts, which Dr. Bosanquet dismisses as of secondary importance.

We cannot, therefore, accept the definition of freedom suggested by Dr. Bosanquet in his new volume. To the question how self-government is possible, he replies that the answer is drawn " from the conception of the general will which involves the existence of an actual community of such a nature as to share an identical mind and feeling. There is no other way of explaining how a free man can put up with compulsion and even welcome it." [1] On the surface this theory is attractive. In an ordered society I am free, though under compulsion, because the will of society is my own will, and the compulsion is exercised by myself upon myself. But these are mere words. The will of society may be radically opposed to my own, and yet I must obey. It may even be my duty to obey, and normally it is so, even though I think the law wrong, because society must be kept together ; and if its deliberate decision is to carry no weight with its dissentient members, profound disorganization must ensue. The evil of one bad law is not, unless in a very extreme case, to be weighed against the evil of diminishing the authority of all law.

The only sense, therefore,· in which I am conforming to my own will, in obedience, is that of two evils I prefer the lesser. If in this I am free, it is not because I am a member of a society like-minded with myself, but simply because I am master of my own actions and can choose, if I will, to abide by the penalties which disobedience will entail. If freedom depended upon identity of will, there would not be much of it in a complex world. In general freedom depends (1) on the defined and restricted use of compulsion. If the state prevents another man from coercing or oppressing me by force or the use of superior economic power, it augments my freedom ; and the uniform compulsion of law is in fact the only known method by which individuals can be assured in the enjoyment of a common liberty from possible oppression by

[1] *Social and International Ideals,* p. 271.

one another. If, on the other hand, the law prevents me
from drinking or compels me to serve in the army, it is
absurd to maintain that it is in these very respects
augmenting my freedom. It may be justified in either
of these actions by other considerations—even by the
consideration of other kinds of freedom—if, for example,
it has been right in judging that compulsory service is
necessary to national freedom. That does not alter the
fact that freedom is impaired at one point even if it is
gained at another, and the man who is compelled against
his will to give up his drink or to join the army is mocked
if you tell him that in doing that which he most resents
his will is free because the decision of society is his own.
Essentially political freedom does not consist in like-
mindedness, but in the toleration of differences ; or,
positively, in the acceptance of differences as contributing
to richer life than uniformity. Freedom, as something
shareable by all members of a community, involves
restraint upon that which prevents such sharing. A
society is on the whole free not because there is in it
little law or much law, but because the law is such as to
secure scope for personal development and free association as a common possession by restricting those developments, and those only, in which the fulfilment of one is
the frustration of another. It is free, not where a common
mind shapes the individual, but where all minds have
that fullness of scope which can only be obtained if certain
fundamental conditions of their mutual intercourse are
maintained by organized effort.[1]

---

[1] Properly interpreted the dictum of Lycophron the Sophist,
that the law is a guarantee of mutual justice, is nearer the truth
than the contrary proposition of Aristotle, that it is such as to
make the citizens good and just (Aristotle, *Politics*, Book III,
ch. ix, § 8). It is not the business of compulsion to make men good
and just, but the guarantee of protection for him who acts justly
is a condition under which men may make themselves good and
just. The state can, however, without serious increase of coercion
apply the resources of organization to secure more positive conditions of development than the mere restraint of injustice, and in
particular it is only the state which can accumulate for social ends

(2) In a second and more specific sense, political freedom implies active citizenship. The claim of the free individual is not the impossible one that the common decision should coincide with his own, but that his decision should be heard and taken into account. He claims his part in the common councils; he takes his share of responsibility. In so far as he makes this claim effective he contributes to the common decision even though in a particular case it goes dead against him. He is free, not because the social will is his own, but because he has as much scope for expression as any one man can have if all are to have it and yet live and act together. More than this is the beginning of tyranny, less is the beginning of slavery.

We cannot, however, do justice to the argument from the likeness between individuals to a common self which actually unites them without reference to the ultimate metaphysical theory of which this transition is a particular case. Let us restate our position as we have maintained it against Dr. Bosanquet's attacks. For us the system of law, the social tradition, is clearly not the product of one will, unless in the imaginary case of an omnipotent despot who imposes a complete system of laws on a subject people. It is rather the product of innumerable wills, acting sometimes in concert, sometimes in opposition to one another, and through their conflicts and combinations issuing in a more or less orderly system, part of which gets itself inscribed on the statute book, while part is incorporated in customs and institutions, and as such passes through generations, conserving its main outlines through long periods, but also subject to expansion, growth and decay. Such is the system of *Recht*, partly moral, partly legal, as understood by the plain man, and as more fully understandable

that large element of wealth which does not depend on the energy of living individuals. It should be remarked in this connection that to restrict the functions of the state is by no means to place a limit on the value of voluntary co-operation, but rather the reverse.

by comparative and historical investigation. If we call it an expression or embodiment of the will, we do not mean by that term a single continuous entity but a universal, that is, something which in reality consists of thousands and millions of wills, all distinct in their existence, though acting on and acted on by one another. But to the Hegelian this statement implies a false view of the universal. We are contending for individuality, for the irreducible distinction between self and others, and we have met some of the arguments directed against that distinction. But now we have admitted a "universal" running through thousands and millions of selves. This admission, according to the idealist, will be fatal to the separateness which we have maintained. The universal for him unites the instances which fall under it just in the manner which we dispute. We have maintained a radical distinction between the identity of character found in different individuals and the identity of continuous existence which constitutes each individual. But the idealist will deny the radical character of this distinction. For him identity is universality, and the two cases of identity that we distinguish are mere specific forms of the universal. We come, therefore, to that theory of the universal which, as we said above, underlies the whole question. This theory is due to Hegel.

What then for Hegel is the universal ?[1] Like other things in his dialectic it can only be understood by surmounting certain false and partial views. Firstly, then, for him the universal is apprehended in contrast with the particular cases in which it is manifested. Thus the colour red is a universal, but it is not the red rose, nor the red cloth, nor the red blood. The red rose is a particular instance of the universal, the red blood is another. Redness, the universal, here is something distinct from, and in a manner opposed to, the cloth and the rose which are red. This is the abstract universal, the universal arrived at by taking away all the particulars in which it appears. But if we take away all the particulars,

[1] See especially *Wissenschaft der Logik*, II, Werke, vol. v. pp. 36–63.

what remains ? If it is neither the red rose, nor the red cloth, nor the red blood nor red anything else, there is no red, nothing appears to remain for the abstract universal, and we seem forced to say that only particulars exist. To escape this difficulty we might perhaps say that red means the common element in the flower, the cloth and the blood. It is the character in which all agree and in which they all share as distinct from the characters in which they differ. But here another difficulty arises. The character of redness is not exactly identical in the different cases. The rose is of one tint or shade, the cloth of another, the blood of a third. The red that is common to all becomes something thinner and more attenuated, of which we can no longer form even a perfectly clear and unambiguous image. If we try to picture the red that is all these things, we stumble, as Hume says, in our minds not upon red in general but some particular shade of red. The difficulty becomes greater the higher we go in the region of abstraction. Red, blue and green are all colours, for example, but what precisely is the colour that is above all, which is not red, nor blue, nor green, nor of any other particular tint ? If we try to think upon these lines, we get into the way of constructing our conception into a kind of mosaic. If colour is an element which is common to two coloured objects, then let us say redness is another element common to one set of coloured objects and distinct from others, and crimson a third element, and luminosity, transparence, opaqueness again further elements, and in this red rose before me several of these particular elements must coexist. Here then in another sense the universal has passed into the particular—the common element, colour, being just one of the constituent parts of the actual colour which is before me. On the other hand, it may be said each of these particulars is also universal, since the colour is common to the entire class of objects, the redness is common to a section of that class, and the particular tint to a smaller section, while certain characteristics like luminosity cut across the distinctions of tint and are common to colours of many different tints. The conclusion of this argument is that the universal as placed in opposition to the particulars, and the particulars placed in opposition to the universal, both involve contradictions. They pass into one another. What is the truth then ? The truth may be seen in this way. Colour is not a distinguishable element common to red, blue, green, etc. It is rather that which is now red, now blue, now green, and so all of them, though it is not all of them at one and the same time and place. Nor is it the sum or totality of them all. This would ultimately be only the collection of all the individual things that are coloured. It is rather the principle that permeates them and that develops itself into the one or the other, and the thought appears to be that, if we had insight into the nature of the universal, we should understand that all these differences arise out of it, as the different organs of the body come from the development of a germ. Hegel expresses this by saying that the true or concrete universal is the individual. By this he does not mean, as he explicitly says, the individual object that our senses appreciate, e.g. the red rose. He means an individuality which permeates or runs through differences of development or expression, so that the differences are related to the universal as are the attributes of an individual thing to the thing itself, or the phases or activities of life to the living being. This distinction is much more plausible as applied to a concept than to the reality to which a concept refers. If one thinks of colour, for example, as an attribute of the material world, to describe it as an individual becomes paradoxical in the highest degree. Colours appear here, there and everywhere under all sorts of changing conditions. There is among them nothing at all resembling the continuity and selfsameness of an individual object. On the other hand, if we think of the concept colour in our mind, we can with more reason regard it as a kind of scheme, which to be realized at all must be filled in in some definite way, but which as a scheme is a permanent unity, and is main-

tained without changing its character through all its
differences of fulfilment. We can then understand that
to say of a thing that it has a particular colour is to place
it in the scope of this scheme, so that we escape from
the difficulty of trying to assign to the term " colour " a
meaning which gives it some definite quality distinguishable from other definite qualities, an attempt which Hegel
rightly says leads us further and further into meaningless
abstraction.

Let us agree then that when we predicate a universal,
e.g. colour, we bring an object into relation with a certain
system which is operative in our minds, and that generally
speaking it is true to say that our concepts are systems of
this kind and systems of such systems. The fallacy in
the Hegelian theory consists in identifying the system of
our thought with the reality to which it refers. The
system of our thought is not identical with the system
of reality, except in the sense that our thought itself
is an event, but has reference to that reality, and reality
itself is not finally intelligible until we take the relation
between it and thought into account by a further and
more comprehensive thought. For example, in the particular case before us we have to recognize that while
in classifying things we form certain systems of universals
and particulars, and while these systems describe things
accurately in one aspect, they do not describe them
under other aspects. If we ask how a thing grows, comes
to be, disappears, for example, we do not get the answer
by exhibiting its place in a classification, but by tracing
its relation to its antecedents, concomitants, consequents
The classificatory system, being all held together in our
thought, has within our thought a unity, even if you
will an individuality. The thinking of it is an individual
act. But the objects to which this unified thought refers
the objects to which the system applies, may be in any
degree scattered through the universe, and devoid of all
the interconnecting threads that make an individual
whole. This then in the last analysis is the fallacy involved in the famous Hegelian doctrine of the concrete

universal. It attributes the unity which belongs to the concept as contained in the act of thinking to the mass of objects to which the concept refers.[1] The reality which the universal describes consists of indefinite numbers of individuals related by identities and differences of character, i.e. by more or less exact resemblance, and not by any substantive or causal continuity such as constitutes the individual.

The confusion of the individual with the universal, however, would never have commanded any acceptance if it had not some plausible basis in fact. What is this' plausible basis ? It is that if you consider the individual under a certain partial aspect, and allowing one fundamental point to drop, its resemblance to the universal leaps to the eyes. Consider the living being, for example, a man. He is in a sense one and the same thing from birth to death, but he is also different from babyhood to youth and youth to manhood ; in a lesser degree, from moment to moment. You have in him a sameness running through difference, which is just what you have in the colour that is common to red, blue and green. He is, moreover, many things in one. He is a thinking, willing being, a spiritual being and a physical being, and his unity pervades all these just as the redness pervades all its tints. Here, too, the question arises whether he is distinct from all the different things that he is, or whether he is all these things regarded as a whole, or whether he is something that is now one and now the other, something which must be the one or the other and which finally manifests itself completely only in the whole series. In all these ways the self-identity of the individual resembles the universal. The fundamental difference is that the individual is continuous throughout his existence. The man's life is not broken, he is always

---

[1] It may be said that every time we make use of the same concept we refer to the same mass of facts. There is thus an identity of reference as well as identity in the thought which makes the reference. But this is not to say that the mass of facts so identified constitute in their internal relations an individual.

there at a given spot at any particular time, and never breaking the continuity of his temporal existence. In speaking of him as an individual we affirm or imply a belief in a substantial continuity. We believe, that is, that what he is at one moment is the basis of what he is at the next, that he has become whatever we find him to be by a process of self-determination. That self-determination is certainly not absolute, for his environment affects him, but there is always an element of self-determination which makes up the continuous thread of his identity. Now as between individuals of the same class, there is no necessary continuity of this kind. Two men may come into relation with one another or they may not. They are nevertheless both members of the same universal and they share a common character which has nothing whatever to do with any substantive continuity. On the other hand—and here is a further source of confusion—as between different individuals there may also be in certain relations important inter-connections, so that while each is an individual and while they constitute members of a class, they may nevertheless be so united as to form a totality which has a certain substantive continuity of its own. Now this is precisely the case with any society. Take a family, for example. All the members are individuals, that is, each has his own substantive continuity. But the family is also a close union of these individuals who in certain relations very intimately affect one another, and so build up a common life. Thus the family is both the class of individuals which compose it, say, all the Thomas Browns— the members of the family Thomas Brown—and also a true individual of a higher order, the family of the Thomas Browns possessing a certain life and unity of its own which makes it behave for many purposes as a single self-contained entity. So regarded, however, the family is not a universal but an individual, though of a different order from the physical individual. It is the confusion of these two aspects of the community which dominates the whole theory of the general will.

Let us see how the logic of it works.   In the first place, the particular, as such, is unreal.   Every particular must be a case of the universal, a manifestation of the universal. Thus the particular man, as particular, has no real existence.   He is only a phase in some universal.   Where then are we to look for the universal ?   Not in his identity of character with other men.   That is the false or abstract universal.   We should look for it in something which is to be called an individual, that must be in some systematic totality, some fabric or union of human beings, self-sustaining, self-determining, a sort of system of wills. Now there are several such systems, but in the Hegelian view that which includes them all is the state, and thus the state is the highest universal to which a particular man belongs as a case or a manifestation, and the will of the state is the real will, the universal will of which particular wills are only incidents or phases.   Accordingly the Hegelian logic abolishes on the one side the independence of the individual living human being, and on the other side the universal ties of identity of character which relate the individual to the human species as a whole, and substitutes for it as the reality the organized body of human beings, which in its highest manifestation is the state.   How far there is an error in fact here, that is, how far it is true that the state is the highest human organization, we need not for the moment inquire.   The point is that by identifying the universal with the individual, Hegel has destroyed the universality of character on which all the highest ethics and the highest religions are founded.   They mean nothing to him because they are mere abstract universals.   At the same stroke he has destroyed the self-dependence of the individual which is the root of freedom, and we can understand why for him all that unsophisticated men call freedom is an irrational and unmeaning caprice, a caprice of the particular, imagining itself to be a substantive reality instead of a mere fold in the garment of the all-covering universal. And yet Hegel's doctrine may be said to have contradicted itself, for if it is true that universality of character rests on membership of some organized whole, then that universality of character, which we do as a matter of fact find in human beings, must imply that humanity is in some sense an organic whole, and the mere fact that we speak of the state as a generic term and recognize that there are many states must imply a universal element connecting them, and therefore must lead to the conception after all of a super-state, at any rate of something that is above all states, comprehending them all and forming an organic unity among them. It is just this organic unity which Hegel denies, recognizing above the state only a spirit of world history which is essentially a process and a process in which states contend and destroy one another, not a unity inspiring them with a single spirit and finding for them also a true freedom in conformity to universal law.[1]

[1] Dr. Bosanquet in his *Principle of Individuality and Value* (Lecture II) recognizes the distinction between generality and what he calls the individuality. He takes the line of depreciating generality, e.g. p. 34, "the most general knowledge . . . must obviously be the least instructive and must have its climax in complete emptiness." To this it may be replied that the law of gravitation is neither uninstructive nor empty, because it applies to all bodies. On the contrary, it was precisely the discovery that it did apply to all bodies, and not only the earth and the objects on its surface, that enabled Newton to draw inferences of extraordinary range and interest. He goes on to argue that "you cannot explain a human body or a steam-engine by classifying the parts in each under their resemblances to one another." This is of course one part of the truth, though not the whole truth. We should not understand the operation of any part of the steam-engine if we could not regard it as an instance of a general law of the operation of bodies precisely similar to that part.

For the rest, Bosanquet's contention only goes to illustrate the difference between the general and the individual, and does not justify the use of the term "universal" derived from generality to characterize the individual. Bosanquet justly finds a certain correspondence, the correspondence noted above, between the individual and the general. "The ultimate principle we may say is sameness in the other. Generality is sameness in spite of the other. Universality is sameness by means of the other" (p. 37). We should say rather generality implies a plurality of objects similar, but not necessarily connected in any other way.

Individuality is a connection, psychical, physical, or whatever it may be, running through many parts and constituting of them one whole. Being unable to deny the distinctness of what we call generality, Bosanquet seems to set himself to minimize its value. He almost seems to scold its obstinacy in remaining a part of the universe. Exclusiveness, we are told, is a kind of minor mark of the individual. It is misleading if too strongly insisted on. It is admitted (p. 104) that a potential generality or repetition is a corollary of the universal infinite experience, " but it is a character of imperfection in such experience and not of perfection . . . why should any being express a second time what has been adequately expressed before ? " So, again, on p. 116, " repetition suggests failure." Is it not rather that the admission of repetition suggests the failure of the theory which identifies the universal with the individual ? A true proposition is not refuted by belittling its significance.

LECTURE IV

THE WILL OF THE STATE

So far we have dealt with two of the three main propositions of the metaphysical theory of the state. Of these three the first is that true individuality or freedom lies in conformity to our real will. The second is that our real will is identical with the general will, and the third—with which we have not yet dealt—is that the general will is embodied more or less perfectly in the state. On analysing the first proposition we found that it rested upon a confusion of two distinct conceptions. The first is the conception of human nature, which is richer and more various than the conscious and deliberate will. The second is the ideal will which would express the practical possibilities of harmony in human nature. The first of these is real, but is neither identical with will nor with rationality. The second is rational will, but is not real. It is something which at best may only be attained by that great transformation of ourselves which is symbolized by the religions in such phrases as "being born again."

The term "real will," therefore, we discarded as a source of nothing but confusion. But having accepted the phrase provisionally from the idealist, we found a further confusion, the argument by which he identifies it with the general will. This argument confused identity of character with identity of continuous existence, the result of which was to set up a common self wherein the difference between one person and another is lost and the whole problem of social relations accordingly is misstated.

These are the two leading fallacies in the metaphysical theory of society, but there is a third fallacy emerging from them which is no less important in its practical applications. That is that the common self or the general will is to be identified with the state. It might be thought that, if we altogether repudiate the conception of a common self, the application falls to the ground along with the principle. None the less the argument needs examination both because it brings out certain elements of fallacy in the central conception and because it bears upon the whole question of the relations of the state to the social life of man.

Waiving all our criticism of the metaphysical identification of the real and the general will, we can understand what is meant by the contention that the full expression of a man's nature is social, that his interests, in the fullest sense of that term, are bound up with those of others and extend in endless ramifications into the texture of the social fabric. But why are they in particular bound up with the state? Is the state then another name for the entire social fabric, for the family, for the mass of one's social interests, for science, art, literature and religion? To the modern mind, at any rate to the non-German mind, the question answers itself in the negative, and outside the metaphysical school most thinkers would regard this as one of the points on which the modern outlook differs essentially from the Greek. To the Greeks [1] the city-state was the focus of all life, and on this fact depended at once the completeness and the harmony of the Greek conception within a certain range and the narrowness and final insufficiency of that range. The self-sufficiency of the city-state was bound up with the failure of the Greeks to achieve a wider nationality and with the undeveloped condition of their religion, which made it impossible to set up a spiritual over the temporal power. Nevertheless, for the Greek thinkers themselves the boundaries to state life were too narrow. Plato

---

[1] I.e. the Greeks of the orthodox tradition. The Cynics and, following them, the Stoics, laid the foundation of the larger view.

might hold that the happiness of his guardians was not to be considered apart from the well-being of the state, to which it was their prime function to contribute, but none the less it is clear that for him the real desires of a trained philosopher are to graze apart in the Elysian Fields of contemplation, and that to recall him to the service of the state is to bring him back into the cave from which he had escaped into the upper air. We do him no wrong, he contends, in demanding this service of the philosopher, for we are merely expecting him to repay what the state has given him in education. None the less it is clear that the philosophic life, which is for Plato the spiritual life, has begun to develop an interest of its own. And so in Aristotle philosophic wisdom is the mistress, not the servant, of the practical wisdom of the statesman, and the theoretic life is primarily concerned with things much higher than man. In the modern world again, apart from Germany, the state had until recent times receded into the background. It was rather the prosaic necessity of social life than the living principle itself. In the metaphysical theory the entire modern tendency is reversed. The state has become, as we have seen, an end in itself, and the reason is that the state is regarded as the sum and substance of our social activities, the organized fabric of civilized life.

Let us follow the reasoning by which Dr. Bosanquet arrives at this conclusion, by which, that is to say, he passes from his conception of the real will as the foundation of our individuality to the state as the supreme object of our allegiance. This transition is introduced by a passage which runs : " The imperative claim of the will that wills itself is our own inmost nature and we cannot throw it off. This is the ultimate root of political obligation." Should we not rather say, a rational harmony of life has an imperative claim on us, and this claim is what we call moral obligation ? Such a proposition would harmonize better with the sentence preceding our quotation, in which rebellion is recognized as a possible duty on the ground that the particular system which claims our obedience may be irreconcilable with the conditions essential to a rational will. If this is understood, it is clear that there is no political obligation that is not subordinate to moral obligation and politics are subordinate to ethics. Thus, the main question of political or social philosophy has to be answered in a manner adverse to those who, like Bosanquet, are seeking to make political philosophy an independent discipline.

None the less Bosanquet goes on to say [1] that the real will is that which thinkers like Rousseau have identified with the state. The justification offered is, that if, starting from the human being, you try to devise that which will furnish him with "an outlet of stable purpose," you will be driven on ".at least as far as the state and perhaps further." The "perhaps further" is a saving clause that may be considered later. Meanwhile we have to deal with Dr. Bosanquet's conception of the state. It is not, we are told, "merely the political fabric, but is the entire hierarchy of institutions by which life is determined, including e.g. the family, trade, the church, the university. It is the structure which gives life and meaning to them all." It is "the operative criticism of all institutions." A perfect conception of the end of the state would mean "a complete idea of the realization of all human capacity." At the same time the state is necessarily force. Force is inherent in the state, being exercised not only in the "restraint of disorderly persons but in the form of instruction and authoritative suggestion to the ordinary law-abiding citizen." It forms a kind of automatism, which underlies our more conscious and intelligent behaviour. But though necessary as a basis of life, force and automatic suggestion are in their nature "contradictory to the nature of the highest self-assertion of mind," not because in the use of force the state is controlling the individual or one man controlling another, for there are no others and there is no individuality opposed to the state, but because the element of force is antagonistic to the best life. It is "a dangerous drug"

---

[1] See *The Philosophical Theory of the State*, p. 149, etc.

which must be administered "as a counter-poison to tendencies which would otherwise give no chance to the logical will." The consequence is that the state, as exercising force, must be rigidly limited in its functions. It must not seek the direct promotion of the good life. " What it can effect is to remove obstacles, to destroy conditions hostile to the realization of the end." Its business is to " hinder hindrances " to the best life.

We have thus a definition of the state, consisting of two clauses, which we must examine separately. As to the first, which identifies the state with the entire social fabric, Dr. Bosanquet seems partly aware that here the state is used in an unusual sense. By the state we ordinarily mean either the government or, perhaps a little more accurately, the organization which is at the back of law and government. The state is the organization of society for the control of its common interests, an organization of which the various departments of law and government are the particular organs. This is something less than the entire fabric. Dr. Bosanquet might argue that there must be organization in order to support the fabric. In advanced societies this is probably true, but (a) many simple societies enjoy a fairly well-ordered fabric of social life without any governmental organization, and others have the very rudest forms of governmental organization. (b) It is quite possible to hold, with the philosophical anarchists, that societies more advanced than our own may achieve an equally good order of social life on a large scale and in complex relations without governmental organization, or at any rate without the use of force. And it is still more possible to hold that the reduction of the use of force to a minimum is a desirable element in the advance of society. If that is so, while it would remain true to identify moral obligation and social obligation, true to maintain that the best life can only be realized in society, it would be untrue to identify that best life with the state. Underlying Bosanquet's account, in fact, there is a serious confusion between the state and society.[1] The state is at present necessary to society, but it is only one of its conditions. The bony skeleton is necessary to the human body and in a sense holds it together, but it is hardly that which constitutes the life of the body, still less that which makes the life of the body desirable and possibly beautiful. Nor is it correct to describe the state as the " operative criticism of institutions." The entire life of society is a whole, of which the parts act and react upon each other. Institutions and customs gradually change and modify each other in large measure without any conscious criticism, just through the actions of individuals seeking to adapt themselves as best they may to their medium. But the bulk of explicit criticism also proceeds through discussion and through all sorts of voluntary agencies, which have not the power of the state, and it is only at certain turning-points that acts of government and legislation have to be called in to make some decisive change. The entire fabric, we may say, carries out its own self-criticism, and once again it is only misleading to identify the entire fabric with a state organization which is only one of its necessary components.

Lastly, much of the organization of life is more extensive than any organized state, and many social divisions cut across state divisions. Bosanquet's own ideas are mostly derived from Germany. The Christian church, in ideal, has always been a cosmopolitan and not a national organization ; and the same is true of other higher religions and of higher ethics and the entire republic of letters, science, philosophy and art. The same is true in another relation of the economic market, which is a world market, and even of economic ideas and to some extent of economic organizations, such as the Socialist International. In a

---

[1] In the Introduction to his second edition (p. xxix) Dr. Bosanquet seems to recognize some of the difficulties of his position, and speaks of a social co-operation which does not belong strictly either to the state or to the private person. If this admission is pressed, it will be found fatal to his first definition of the state as the entirety of the social fabric.

word, the state, as an organization, is a mere means to an end. It is one of the ways in which human beings are grouped. In its present form it is the product of certain modern conditions not of very long standing and probably not destined to very long endurance. To confuse the state with society and political with moral obligation is the central fallacy of the metaphysical theory of the state.

The truth is that Bosanquet's double definition of the state, on the one hand as the operative criticism of institutions and on the other hand as force, is an abortive union of two radically opposed conceptions. Criticism is the very opposite of force. It is something essentially spiritual. It belongs to the mind, it demands the maximum of freedom. It lives in discussion unconstrained. It is no respecter of persons. It fills up no forms. It is bound by no traditions. It is free as air. Force, on the other hand, moves on the solid ground. As law, its principles must be defined and established, executed by authority, regardless of finer meanings and subtle differences. It closes its ear to discussion, which is taken to be complete at the moment when force is decided upon. Human society has not often found it possible to dispense with force because, though mind is free as air, the body to which mind is attached must have the solid rock to stand on, and men have judged an imperfect order better than no order at all. The modern mind, aware of this contrast, of the necessity of force and of the threat which it contains to the life of the spirit, has sought unceasingly for some theory of the limits of force, has asked itself anxiously how much and how little is the state bound to exact from its members. But the idealistic theory, far from illuminating, serves to confuse the entire issue. In Dr. Bosanquet's presentation in particular we get a most confusing oscillation between the two principles conveyed by his definition. If we ask about the duties of the individual to the state, we find him leaning on the state as operative criticism. The duty of the individual appears to be absolute, his very personality is merged in the state, and for the same reason, as we shall see presently, the state has no authority over it, but is the final form of human association. If, on the other hand, we ask about the duties of the state to the individual, what it can do for the promotion of the well-being of its members, we find that the state is only force and all its action is limited by the clumsiness and externality of compulsion. It cannot directly promote freedom, but only hinder hindrances.[1] By playing between these two meanings, we get the worst of both worlds ; on the one side a state which absorbs and cancels individual personality and knows little or no morality in its external relations ; and on the other side the social morals of the Charity Organization Society, a state which cannot actively promote the well-being of its members, but can only remove obstructions and leave to them a fair field in which to run the race. The truth is that the state is only one element in the society of humankind. It is an organization which men have built up, partly with conscious purpose, but largely through a clash of purposes which has settled down into an order exhibiting some

[1] The hindrance of hindrances is indeed so vague an expression that almost anything can be extracted out of it, e.g. we are told (p. 172) that the state hinders illiteracy by compelling education. When formulæ are so stretched it is a sign of something wrong in the theory underlying them. In public education two functions of the state are involved. (1) Compulsion, which is necessary to secure the right of the child against a neglectful parent, a right which, like all rights, is a condition of social welfare, and (2) the organization of public resources for a public object. We too often tend to think of such organization in terms of compulsion because it involves taxation. But taxation is not adequately conceived when thought of as the compulsory taking from individuals of property which is absolutely theirs. There are social factors in production, and therefore elements due to society rather than to the individual, which can only be secured for the community by the mechanism of the state. Taxation is a very rough, and in practice not always an equitable, method of securing these elements of collective wealth, but to secure them for common objects and organize their application is one of the functions of the state which is entirely missed by Dr. Bosanquet's account.

permanence, but constantly threatened with more or less revolutionary changes. In this order there is nothing sacrosanct. On the contrary, government, law and the institutions lying behind and supporting them are far from being the most successful of the experiments of mankind. They call aloud for radical criticism, and to deify them is to establish false gods, gods who at the present time figure as veritable Molochs before whom our sons are made to pass in millions through the fire.

But there is a further point. Let us for the moment take the state in the extended sense which the Hegelians assign to it. Let us regard it as the entire fabric of existing society. What then is the nature of our obligations to this fabric ? What is its authority and its claim upon our reason and conscience ?

The idealist maintains that the customs, traditions and institutions of society are the expression of an objective mind or spirit. These are contrasted by Hegel with the abstractions which the subjective reason evolves, and he speaks of the French Revolution as a monstrous display of the result of overthrowing the given and existing constitution of a great actual state, and endeavouring to make the mere supposedly rational the basis of a constitution in place of the historic reality. " Against the principle of the individual will we are to remind ourselves of the fundamental conception that the objective will is rational in its concept, whether it is recognized by individuals and willed with pleasure or not." [1] In the same way [2] Dr. Bosanquet tells us that in the system of institutions we have objective mind :

" We have only to repeat what many great men have explained at length, that in this world of content, the work of thinking will, we have in an external and factual form the body and substance of thinking will itself. Here is its concrete and actual content, what it finds to affirm in its volition from moment to moment, what forms the steps and systematic connections by which its

---

[1] *Phil. des Rechts*, p. 308.
[2] *Principle of Individuality*, p. 112.

self-expression from day to day is linked with—enters into—the total world of its satisfaction in a law which is at once its own nature and a high expression of the absolute. What a contrast with the abstract formulas of Hedonist or intuitionist axioms ! "

It comes then to this. The attempts of thinking men to conceive and establish a rational order of society are mere fantasies of the subjective reason. The actual institutions of a given society are the objective reason. Society, any society it would seem that ever has been, is a higher embodiment of reason than any of the conscious reflections of the philosopher or statesman. When we think of the actual inconsistencies of traditional social morality, the blindness and crudity of law, the elements of class-selfishness and oppression that have coloured it, the mechanical dullness of state institutions even at their best, the massive misery that has lain at the foundation of all historic civilizations, we are inclined to say that no mere philosopher, but only the social satirist, could treat this conception as it deserves.

But we must endeavour to understand the conception on which it rests and the reason why it is wrong. For this purpose we may start from the passage in which Dr. Bosanquet sums up the theory of state action in the Rousseauite formula " sovereignty is the exercise of the general will." He justifies this by saying that all state action is general ; that is, it consists in customs, laws and institutions of general application. And, secondly, by saying that " all state action is at bottom the exercise of the will," and this is " the real will." To say that state action is general and that it is willed, is not, however, the same thing as to say that it is the exercise of a general will. The distinction seems dialectical, but it touches the substance of the question. It is true that laws and customs are general, but, as general, how far are they willed ? How far, that is, are they the products of an intelligence that has clearly foreseen all their bearings ? How far are they the products of a unitary will that has taken all social life into its account as a single coherent system and thought out the bearings of one part upon another ? The answer to this question is, not very far, hardly at all. The life of society is not the product of coherent thinking by a single mind. On the contrary, many customs and institutions, which make up social life, have grown up in a detached, sporadic, unconscious, often unreasonable fashion, and even the more conscious and deliberate ones are rather efforts to correct some particular mischief, amend some particular anomaly, than clearsighted applications of a governing principle to social life as a whole. And so, secondly, when Dr. Bosanquet says that society rests on will, the answer is rather that it rests on wills. We seldom find in a great society, as a whole, a will comparable to that in you or me relative to our personal ends. When I will a thing I clearly see what I mean to do. I have weighed it in the balance with its advantages and disadvantages, brought it into relation with emotions and desires, some of which it may satisfy while others it may thwart, and I have in the result identified myself as a whole with a particular course or particular object, whatever it may be. It is rare that society does anything of this kind collectively. The nearest approach is found in a war, and for instructive reasons. It is in a war, when pitted against others, that the millions of men, constituting a society, find themselves to be most distinctly an individual whole contending with other individuals, when they must win or lose as a whole and make up their minds definitely whether the struggle with all its losses is worth continuing.

In the internal developments of a nation, where no such external pressure exists, it is rare to find decisions clearly taken by the people as a whole. True, in a democratic nation laws are in the end passed by parliamentary majorities, which may and should represent the majority of the nation, but any one who considers the actual process of legislation, the steps by which a bill reaches the form in which it is ultimately inscribed in the statute book, to say nothing of the form in which it is really applied by the courts, must recognize that

6

it is a process made up of innumerable conflicts of innumerable wills, in which there is every sort of give and take, compromise and adjustment, contrasting very clearly with the simple and crisp decisions of an individual mind. It is true that with political education and the development of effective democracy the sphere of intelligent social control is extended, and it would be a sound statement of the democratic ideal to say that it conceives a possible society regulating its common life by common consent, in which a larger and larger proportion of its members actively participate until a position be reached in which society would control itself as simply and effectively as the individual controls himself. This is an ideal, and not one very near to realization. Of the social structure of any state that exists it is generally untrue to say that it is clearly conceived by the minds of the majority of those who live in it, and it is profoundly untrue to regard the actual development of any society, as we have known it in history, as the product of an intelligent purpose alone.[1]

Too often it is not the state as a whole which sets definite ends before itself. In the normal development of peace-time, and for that matter even in the concentrated purpose of war-time, there are many sections within the state which have each for itself a general will, far more properly so called because much more clearly conscious and united than any will which permeates the state as a whole. The actual institutions of society have been in large measure determined by class conflicts, struggles of churches, racial wars, and everywhere 'here are the marks of the struggles. If and in so far as there is any meaning in the term " general will " at all, there are many general wills within the state, and too often the institutions of society are just the result of the victory, resting not on logic but on superior organization, which one of these wills has attained

[1] It is remarkable that in another connection Dr. Bosanquet writes, " Nothing is properly due to finite mind, as such, which never was a plan before any finite mind."—*Principle of Individuality*, p. 152.

over others. Green, who, whatever the idealistic basis
of his theory, retained his fundamental humanity, saw
that there were instances in which it was a mere mockery
to describe the institutions of a state as the realization
of freedom for all its members, and contended forcibly
that the requirements of the state have " largely arisen
out of force directed by selfish motives." It is inter-
esting to see how Dr. Bosanquet deals with these uncom-
fortable criticisms. He partly admits their truth, but
turns the edge of them by insisting on a rational element
running through the selfishness and shortsightedness of
the particular wills that have gone to make up the social
order, dwelling at the same time on the potential and
implied recognition of the interests of society in the minds
of its selfish members. If state organization were radically
and fundamentally well-meaning, and marred only by
imperfection of insight and inadequacy of means to an
end, this answer might be sufficient, but in so far as
civilized society throughout its history has in very large
measure consisted in the imposition upon the many of
an order of life wherein the essential benefits are reaped
by the few, Bosanquet fails to meet the real point of
Green's challenge. We come back again to the central
point that the institutions of society are not the outcome
of a unitary will but of the clash of wills, in which the
selfishness and generally the bad in human nature is
constantly operative, intermingled with but not always
overcome by the better elements.

The point is very clearly seen in a Note in the chapter
which follows on p. 296 as to the term " the mind of
society." " I neglect for the moment the difference
between the mind of society and mind at its best. The
difference is practically considerable, but I shall attempt
to make it appear in the course of the present chapter
to be a difference of progress and not of direction." The
comment to be made on this is that the difference is so
fundamental that it cannot be neglected even for a moment
without risk of the most serious fallacy. So far as the
metaphorical expression " mind of society " can be

justified at all, it must be said that it is mind at a very low stage of its development. In other words, social institutions may be regarded as outcomes of a mentality of a kind, but that mentality, when viewed in relation to the objects which it has to subserve, is of a low type compared, let us say, to the mentality of a mother considering the welfare of her child. A good mother will act with a clear vision and an unselfish prompting for the child's good, unmixed with thought of her own. If there were a social will which so conceived the good of all the vast numbers of human beings affected by social institutions, it would be on a level with the mind of the mother, and be something much greater than her mind in proportion to the vastness of its object. But just because the object is so vast and so impersonal, the " social mind " falls lamentably short in attaining it, and we may rather compare social mentality to the gropings of one of the lower orders of animals which shifts itself from side to side, straining after a momentary adjustment which it does not even distinctly conceive. But even in this image we have somewhat overestimated the mentality of society, for the animal is after all one, and suffers discomfort as a whole. We might think rather of the separate tentacles of a sea-anemone, of which experiment has shown that one may be educated to reject a non-nutritious object while another is still seeking to grasp it.

Dr. Bosanquet speaks of an ideal that one hopes may be realized somewhere on the far horizon of human progress, but one of the surest ways of arresting that progress is to speak as though that horizon had already been reached.

We have quoted above the passage in which Dr. Bosanquet speaks of the habits and institutions of any community as " so to speak the standing interpretation of all the private wills which compose it." Though an imperfect representation of the real will " because every set of institutions is an incomplete embodiment of life," they are " very much more complete than the explicit ideas which at any given instant move any individual mind in volition." The logic of such passages is this. The real will would work itself out in a harmony of actions. The institutions of society produce some kind of order and so are a partial embodiment of the real will. But (a) when it is said that these institutions are more complete than the explicit ideas of individual minds, it seems to be forgotten that they may also be very much less explicit, much less reasoned out, much less clearly reduced to principle than the ideas of a reflecting mind. An individual mind may not be able to grasp, and certainly could not create the complex of institutions and customs that is the work of many millions of minds, but these complex customs have in very large measure grown up in a groping, unreflective fashion, with little or no reference to any general and comprehensive principle of social well-being, and to grasp such principles is the work of the reflective individual consciousness, which moves on a much higher level than the general will, if we adopt for the moment Dr. Bosanquet's name for the complex of psychological forces which generate and maintain a tradition. (b) When Dr. Bosanquet speaks of the institutions of a community as the standing interpretation of all the private wills that compose it, he speaks as though all society were a real working democracy. Of the working of society as a whole this is invariably untrue. In ordinary workaday life the individual man has simply to accept the fabric within which he finds himself a part. Many features in it he may resent or dislike, but he has simply to deal with them as best he may. And wherever a community is governed by one class or one race, the remaining class or race is permanently in the position of having to take what it can get. To say that the institutions of such a society express the private will of the subject class is merely to add insult to injury. It was not by the private wills of the peasantry of England that their land was enclosed. It may be said they did not revolt. The answer is that they could not do so with effect, and that if, in Bosanquet's language, their real will means the expression of what they really wished, they would have revolted and prevented it.   The actual institutions of a society are not the imperfect expression of a real will, which is essentially good and harmonious, but the result into which the never-ceasing clash of wills has settled down with some degree of permanency, and that result may embody much less of justice, morality and rationality than the explicit ideas of many an individual mind.

As to the problems of social philosophy, Dr. Bosanquet has a very easy solution.   " The end of the state, as of the individual, is the realization of the best life."   As to this we may all agree, but Dr. Bosanquet proceeds, " The difficulty of defining the best life does not trouble us because we rely throughout on the fundamental logic of human nature *qua* rational."   Yet it is supposed to be the object of philosophy to exhibit this logic, and the despised " theorists of the first look " have made it their business to do so.   They have confessed that the object of the state is to consist in realizing a good life, and they have sought by reason, that is, by actually following, as far as in them lies, the logic of human nature, to ascertain the principles of the best life and the way in which these principles should be realized in society.   Dr. Bosanquet professes to skip all that, which is in effect to take the substance out of social philosophy.   The underlying explanation of this is the fundamental conservatism of the idealistic attitude.   The idealist sees the good or the rational realized in the existing order, not perfectly, he would admit, but in its essential outlines.   The rationalist approaches the existing order with an unbiassed mind, and testing it by inquiry, he finds in it elements of radical good and radical evil blended.   The reason for this blend goes right back to the roots of social and mental evolution ; it rests on the fact that society is precisely not the outcome of one real will but of millions and millions of wills through the generations.   In these millions and millions of wills there is a social element working.   There are elements of idealism, sparks of justice, uniting threads of human kindness, and there are also selfishness and vanity and pride and hardness, corporate and collective as well as individual, and these elements acting upon one another make up the piebald pattern of human society.

To sum up. The conception of social institutions as objective reason annuls the function of reason in human society. It teaches the man who would think about social order, who would try to work back from it to some set of ethical principles commending themselves to rational reflection, that in seeking to reason he is sinning against reason. He is to realize that in society he is in the presence of a being infinitely higher than himself, contemplating a reason much more exalted than his own. His business is not to endeavour to remodel society,[1] but to think how wonderfully good and rational is the social life that he knows, with its Pharisees and publicans, its gin-palaces, its millions of young men led out to the slaughter, and he is to give thanks daily that he is a rational being and not merely as the brutes that perish. And, having so given thanks, he is to do his duty in that state of life to which it has pleased the state-god to call him. The root of this conception is the common self. It is the notion that one mind, one will vastly greater than yours or mine, constitutes the life and directs the course of each organized society. Against this conception both philosophy and science may protest, philosophy claiming the ultimate right of reason, the conscious reason which each individual may and must acquire for himself, to criticize the established fact and to form its own ideal for the best life that is within its power; science on the ground that human society, as it has grown up, is the product of unnumbered wills, of their clash as well as their harmony. We may say truly that ethical philosophy cannot construct the state without reference to the established fact. We must start from the place in which we find ourselves. We must understand society, know how it works, before we can improve it. Science must be added to philosophy before we can have a social

[1] For Hegel philosophy comes after reality, and has merely to interpret it.—*Phil. des Rechts*, p. 20.

art ; and if this had been their line of criticism, much of what the idealists from Hegel onwards have had to say about the shortsighted revolutionaries might have been justified. But this is not their point of view. They use the failures, the wrongs, and the wilful dogmatism of some social philosophers to discredit philosophy itself, and with it all genuine reason.

But now, it may be asked, if we deny the ultimate authority of law, custom and tradition, what do we set in its place ? We make political obligation subordinate to moral obligation. But what is moral obligation ? The details of political obligation are written down in a code of law or incorporated in judicial decisions, or more vaguely, but still with sufficient precision, in the customs and understandings of society. This is the concrete rule of life which Hegel calls *Sittlichkcit*. Apart from some fringes of uncertainty, where there is a latitude of interpretation, it is something objective and impersonal. When a man refuses to recognize it, on what authority does he fall back ? In many historic cases the answer has been that in place of the law of the state or the custom of society, a rebel has appealed to the law of God or the church. In the case of the church he is appealing from one society to another society, from the secular to the spiritual, from the supposedly lower, therefore, to the supposedly higher. And, if the appeal is not to the church but to God, it has been the belief of many men that the written word of God is no less clear or certain than the written law of the state. In the case of the appeal to the church we have a conflict, not between one organized society and the individual, but between one organized society and another ; and historically men have attempted to solve the difficulties which have arisen on one of three possible lines, by making the church subordinate to the state, by making the state subordinate to the church, or by an attempt to delimit the affairs of the church and the state, a compromise which has on the whole been accepted in the modern world, which in the main has found the means of compelling the citizen to render unto Cæsar the things that are Cæsar's, while allowing him to render unto God the things which he believes to be God's. Both in practice and theory this demarcation, if not finally satisfactory, is at least a better solution than either of the alternatives. For, on the one side, in so far as the church rules by a spiritual influence, its authority is morally the higher. Every church worthy of the name is in principle that which the idealist falsely maintains the state to be: a society founded upon principles laying down what are believed to be the conditions of a good and righteous life. If any church had in fact succeeded in grasping the entire spiritual meaning of life, its authority would be absolute and it would absorb the state as a subordinate branch. But as churches, like other human associations, are fallible, and as they are founded upon principles which are obscure and upon which, therefore, men differ, it has not in point of fact been found possible to place government and citizenship in a free society on the basis of a common acknowledgment of certain dogmas of religion. Thus the maintenance of certain common requisites of social life has either been kept out or has passed out of the hands of the church. With regard to these common requisites, the state will exert an authority against or over the authority of any church to which its members may happen to belong. Hence the necessity of defining as closely as possible the common requisites for the sake of which the state must exercise compulsion even in defiance of spiritual authority. (1) The state, as the organized power of the community, is the guarantor of the rights of all its members and will not allow a wrong to be done to any one of them in the name of any other authority. The state is fallible and may err in its definition of rights as in other things, but it is its business to form the best judgment in this matter according to its lights, and, having formed it, to enforce it. (2) The state operates through universal laws, and it may find that objects essential to the common welfare, even to the common existence, cannot be secured if exceptions are admitted in such cases. Again, as a guardian of the common existence, the state is within its right in exacting conformity. The other side of this principle, perhaps more readily forgotten, is that it is only when universal conformity is provedly necessary that compulsion is justified in overriding religious conviction.

But let us assume bona fides on both sides, and let us suppose that every effort has been made on the part of the state to reduce its requirements to its lowest terms, and on the part of the church to equate its spiritual teaching with the temporal duties of the citizen. None the less, as we are dealing with fallible human beings in a complex world, there is always a marginal possibility of conflict. In case of such conflict it is not possible to say a priori that either the state is right or the church is right. It is a case of one association of fallible human beings against another. Each owes a certain consideration to the other. The state is bound to respect religious conviction, the church to have regard for the value of law and order in society. But when the last word has been said and those responsible for the state can see, no other way to the preservation of social order or national existence but the enforcement of a given law upon all citizens regardless of creed, then those responsible for the state, and all citizens as owing allegiance to the state, are bound to act in accordance with their final judgment, fallible as it may be, of what is necessary to social preservation. And similarly, the churchman, when he has taken the state's point of view fully into account and weighed it in the scale against his own law, if he can find no way of escaping from the spiritual duty incumbent upon him, seems bound to take the risks, moral as well as legal, of disobedience

There is indeed a court of appeal. There is an objective moral order underlying all disputes, an order which if once apprehended would settle all controversies. But, unless and until this objective order is apprehended and agreed upon by men, moral conflicts will not cease. Appeal indeed is always open until agreement is reached.

New facts and new arguments are never barred, and no opinion is to be silenced ; but if no clear verdict is collected and both parties remain firm in their conviction, there is nothing for it but that the case should go to the ordeal, the barbaric ordeal of endurance. That this is a satisfactory solution no one would contend, but it is better to recognize frankly that in the region of ultimate moral conflict each party is bound by its own conviction than to obscure the issue by such subterfuges as the contention that true freedom would consist in subordination.

What has been said of the possible conflict between church and state, which now has for the most part only a historic interest, is also applicable in principle to conflicts between the state and the individual which have a present, and, it is to be feared, a future significance of a tragic kind. The difference is that where the churchman pleads the recognized law of an organized body, the individual pleads his conscience. We are thus brought to the question of the rights of conscience, their reality and their limitations. In a simpler time, and in our own time to the more simple-minded men, conscience can be taken as the voice of God within and its deliverances may be fortified by an appeal to the written word of God without. So conceived, conscience is as much above state law in authority as it is below it in power ; but in a sceptical age men realize more fully that there is a subjective element in conscience. Consciences differ, and the word of God, even if we take it to be an inspired document, is manifestly liable to the greatest diversities of interpretation. What I call my conscience is my final judgment, when all things bearing on the situation have been summed up, of my right and my duty. This judgment, common experience and psychological analysis will alike show, is in part dependent on idiosyncrasies of my own, on special experiences that have impressed me, on emotional tendencies that make me attach more weight to one thing and less to another, on partial application of principles, on obscurity of ideas. Conscience, then, would seem to have but little final authority. It falls short of the objectivity attached to law and the social tradition. How can it be set up as a standard of nonconformity in some vital matter? The answer of the individual in the first place is that conscience may be a poor thing, but it is his own ; and the answer of the moral law must be that, though there may be many errors incident to the principle that men should do ultimately what is right in their own eyes, yet, if they do anything else than what is right in their own eyes, there is no moral law at all. Moral action is action in conformity with an inward principle, an action that the agent considers to be right and performs because he believes it to be right. If people are required to give up what they consider to be right, morality is annulled. May a man act, then, without regard to law or the judgment of others? On the contrary, what experience in practical matters will often teach him is that others are wiser than he, what morality will teach him is that the law which is right for him must in principle be a law of universal application, holding for all men similarly situated. What duty and practical sense will combine to show him is that he is a man among many, a member of an organized society, and if morality teaches him that he must do what he thinks good, it inculcates at the same time that what is good for him must be a common good. Nevertheless, he is in the end to stand by his judgment of the nature of the common good and the means by which it is to be realized. Once given, as in the case of the churchman, that he has well and truly weighed all that law and society have to say, that he has taken into account the limitations of his own experience and the fallibility of his own judgment as one weak individual opposed perhaps to the millions of all organized society ; when he has then asked himself frankly if it is not his final duty to waive his first judgment, to stifle the inward prompting from respect for an outward order built up by the organized efforts of men, valuable in itself and endangered if any one rebels against it ; when, having duly tested the case in a spirit of humility, he has nevertheless come finally to the conclusion that, all said and done, the obligation is upon him to disobey, then, as a free agent, nonconformity is his only course.

It should be observed that when we say he is right in following this course our proposition has two meanings, which must not be confused. To disentangle them, let us for a moment put ourselves on the side of the state. Let us suppose the state is justified in its behest, that if we were gods knowing good and evil, we should give our verdict on the side of the state, then in that sense and from that point of view, the nonconformist is clearly wrong just as, if the verdict were given the other way, he would be clearly right. But even in the case where he is wrong in one sense he is also right in another. It is right that he should do what he thinks right although, as it happens, he thinks wrong ; the ultimate reason of this is that, though by so acting he is wrong on occasion, if he acted otherwise as a matter of principle he would never do right at all, and if every one so acted, right and wrong as moral terms would disappear. And by the same reasoning, the state, in so far as it holds itself trustee for the final good of society, will recognize that it is better for its members to be free men who will from time to time give trouble by mistakes of judgment, than conforming persons with whom everything is smooth because they never think at all. For this reason the state will avoid coercion of conscience up to the last resort, but once again, as in the case of the church, we have to admit as correlative to the ultimate right of conscience, an ultimate right of coercion. The state, a fallible organization of fallible men, has nevertheless to act according to its lights for the safety of the whole. Where it can see no escape from a universal rule, where this rule would be frustrated by individual acts of disobedience, where by disobeying A would in its judgment do a wrong to B, there in the end it has to exercise constraint, and there seems to be no appeal. The judgment of mankind may ultimately say that the state was wrong, but even so it will have to extend to the state the same charity which

is due to the nonconforming individual. If the state
acted bona fide by its best lights, it could do no better.
What the state has no right to do is to exercise cruelty
or insult. It has no right to place the conscientious
objector on a level with the felon or to use the weapon
of derision, contumely and degradation.[1]

It may be asked finally whether the duty which we
have recognized in a subordinate place of surrendering
our judgment to that of others and in particular to the
organized will of society, is not of a more authoritative
character. If conscience is not the voice of God, why
should we attach so much importance to what one or
two individuals happen to think? Does not the wisdom
of our ancestors, enshrined in institutions, supply a better
test of truth? What social value attaches to individuality? The answer is that the individual, fallible and
weak as he may be in his isolation, is still the centre of
a rich diversity of relations, of which his relation to a
society claiming his allegiance is only a part. The
organized system of life only covers a portion of the
ground. What is recognized and formulated is but a
fragment of living experience. Every individual draws
from deeper wells of being than those revealed in current

[1] In the actual controversy with the conscientious objectors to
military service the state has definitely put itself in the wrong.
For a mechanism was devised for exempting the small number
of men whose principles were perfectly well known and who could
not be expected to change them on demand without incurring
personal dishonour. This mechanism was such as to leave the
general obligation to service untouched, and the refusal of the handful of objectors in no way obstructed the organization of the
man-power of the country as a whole. But the machinery was
not consistently applied, with the result that some conscientious
objectors were left unmolested and others sentenced to long and
repeated terms of rigorous imprisonment. This is state action
at its worst, arbitrary, inconsistent and vindictive, and persistent
in its wickedness. I rejoice to read in Dr. Bosanquet's new volume
that "the conscientious objector will follow his conscience to the
end, and if we believe him to be sincere we all respect him for it."
I rejoice, but with some bewilderment, for I cannot fuse the spirit
of this remark (and of some others in *Social and International Ideals*)
with the general spirit of *The Philosophical Theory of the State*.

speech and custom. If we do not any longer think of him as directly in converse with God, we can think of him as a part of nature, the product physically and spiritually of a long ancestral line of development, susceptible to emotional and ideal suggestions from all manner of experience. If it is through all these that error comes, it is always through one individual that each new truth first comes, and it is better for society in the end to be exposed to many errors than to run the risk of losing one truth. Given freedom of discussion and even of experiment in living, errors will reveal themselves for what they are, and sometimes, the husk being stripped off, the kernel of truth will be found within them. What the state has to prevent is the emergence of error is such a form as will destroy society, and that is one reason why the dictum of Hegel is profoundly false that the claim to say and write what you will is parallel to the right to do what you will. If nonsense is freély uttered and freely controverted, it will reveal that it is nonsense. What is true will be found not by silencing error but by confuting it, and in its regard for the individual, however troublesome he may be, the state is conserving the conditions of its own progress. The line between speech and action is not always clear, but the difference of principle is not obscure. A man may claim a right which invades the rights of another or paralyses the organized effort of the community. In the former case the right claimed by A is resented as a wrong by B, and the state is in its proper sphere in judging between them, deciding where right lies and seeing the limit is not overstepped. In the latter the recalcitrance of one man might wreck the purpose, perhaps endanger the safety of a community. The community has a right through the state to protect itself against such injury. Where both these grounds fail the state has no right to put compulsion upon conscience. Where there is no question of conscience the limits of state activity are matters of convenience, good organization and the relative merits of individual spontaneity and collective regulation

LECTURE V

THE idealistic conception of the state has sometimes figured as an organic theory of society. In the form given to it by Green this description is not unjust, for to Green, the ethical basis of the state is a common good, which at the same time is the good of each individual citizen. The state rests, for Green, on a mutual recognition of rights, rights being for each the conditions under which he can live the best life. We have here beyond doubt the elements of an organic theory, or, if the term be preferred, of a harmony between the state and the individual. Now such a harmony, it is only fair to say, is contemplated by Hegel himself as the true relation between the state and the individuals which compose it. The individual, he says,[1] "must, in the fulfilment of his duties, in some way or other at the same time find his own interest, his satisfaction, and from his relations in the state a right must accrue to him whereby the universal interest (*Sache*) is his own particular interest. The particular interest should not actually be set aside or altogether suppressed, but put into agreement with the universal, whereby both it and the universal are sustained." And again, "All turns on the unity of the universal and particular in the state"; and in this the modern state is distinguished from the ancient. This points to the true ideal, but unfortunately there is nowhere in Hegel a clear distinction between the ideal and the actual. The idealistic habit of talking of "the state" as though there were only one type that

[1] *Phil. des Rechts*, p. 317.

is real, while all existing instances may be regarded as merely casual and secondary aberrations, bars the way to a frank exposition of the contrast of which in experience we are painfully aware between that which might be and that which is.

Hegel recognizes bad states, but he deals with them very summarily. "The state (p. 339) is actual (*wirklich*) and its actuality consists in this, that the interest of the whole realizes itself in the particular aims. . . . In so far as this unity is absent, a thing is not actual, even if its existence might be assumed. A bad state is such a one as merely exists. A sick body also exists, but it is no true reality." Thus in place of asking to what extent it is really true that individual and universal interests coincide and what we are to do when they are palpably in conflict, how we are to cure the sick state and what is the duty of the individual when he finds himself unable to do so, we find the whole question waved aside by a radically unsound distinction between reality and existence. A sick body, as the sufferer has too much reason to know, is as hard a reality as a sound body, and if Hegel's criterion of reality were to be accepted, no state that is or has ever been is real. Regard the harmonic conception of society as an ideal and you give us something to work for, regard it as something actually realized and you confuse every issue of practical reform and theoretic right. In particular, in the notion that the state has the authority of a common self standing above the individual, we have a principle which may but too easily develop into a complete denial of the organic conception, because, instead of recognizing that the value of the state lies in its service to the harmonious development of all its component members, it subordinates that development in each and therefore in all to the fictitious whole which contains them but is not them.

Had Hegel carried through the organic conception of the state, he would have found room for the conception of liberty, equality and democracy ; but his state system is a negation of all these. By an inconsistency which goes to the root of his whole metaphysical argument, he suddenly declares that the personality of the state is only real as a person, a monarch (p. 359). The monarch at one point appears as little more than the figure-head. If the constitution is fixed and formed, he has often nothing to do but to sign his name (p. 363). It is wrong to demand objective qualities of the monarch. He has only to say " yes " and to dot the *i* (p. 365). And so there is no objection to his being chosen in " a natural way " through natural birth (p. 364). An election of a ruler by popular choice will be something dependent on the opinions and expressions of the many and is generally opposed to the idea of " *Sittlichkeit* " (p. 367). Yet this monarch, who is only to dot the *i* and requires no objective qualities, may in short be a fool or a brute, is to have the choice of counsellors responsible for the government, in his unlimited caprice (*Willkür*, p. 370).

To ask for consistency in these deliverances would no doubt be censured by Hegel as a demand of reflective reasoning. But if the king may be a fool, whose caprice may yet determine the government of the state, the opinion of the people is allowed no such latitude. The people, without the monarch and the articulation of the whole into ranks, classes, corporations and so forth, is the formless mass which is no longer a state (p. 360). That the organization of the people as a voting power might be a necessary corrective of the social divisions incident to a large and developed society, does not seem to have suggested itself to Hegel. The people, as far as that word expresses a special portion of the members of the state, is that portion which does not know what it wants (p. 386). Special interests should be represented, but to let the many elect representatives is to give hostages to accident (p. 398). Goethe is quoted with approval as saying that " the masses can fight. There they are respectable. Their judgment is miserable," or, as the modern German phrase puts it, they are " cannon fodder." Public opinion always contains an underlying truth, but is always false in its expression. It must be as much despised as respected (p. 403). It contains all error and truth, and to find the truth in it is the work of the great man (p. 404). We must not ask the people themselves what they think apparently, but we must tell them what they think. The principal guarantee of the freedom of the press is the guarantee of contempt. The claim to say and write what one will is parallel to the freedom to do what one will (p. 404). The landowning class is alone suited for participation in political power on account of its property, which secures it both against the government and against the uncertainty of trade (pp. 391–2).

From all this we can see how much participation in the general will means for the ordinary individual in the Hegelian scheme. Those who have taken the Hegelian conception as a stable framework for democracy on the ground that simple membership of the community involves a share in the common self, would be condemned by Hegel himself for adherence to an abstract conception ; even the rational, thinking element within the common man is to be elicited for him by the great man, the ruler or the law. He is to be told what he thinks. It may be admitted that these are not necessary consequences of the doctrine of the common self ; they are not even natural consequences. It would be more reasonable to expect of a thinker who started from the spiritual unity of society that he would, with Green, insist upon including the humblest along with the highest in the moral unity and would emphasize that which the common man has to contribute no less than that which he has merely to accept. He would, in the spirit of Green, lay bare the elements of a higher meaning, the filaments, however incompletely developed, that bind the humble man to the whole to which he belongs, the half-understood emotions and desires in which higher and wider purposes are implied. It would be unfair to deny that in Hegel himself there are hints of such a development of thought. That they are not carried out is a consequence traceable in the end to that conception of will as having its freedom in determination by a principle rather than in a harmony of impulses which we found to be the starting-point of the Hegelian conception of the state.

The state being the individual writ large, its own independence is the primary condition of its internal life and indeed of its freedom (p. 409). And for this reason it imposes an absolute sacrifice on the individual when it is necessary to maintain it. Hegel finds in this circumstance a contradiction of the view that the end of the state is the security of life and property of individuals, because he says this security would not be reached by the sacrifice of that which was to be secured (p. 410), as though the life of some might not willingly be offered up for the well-being of others, However, in the security of the state lies the " ethical moment " of war, which is to be regarded as not an absolute evil or as merely an external accident (p. 410). Its good side is that it compels us to risk life and property. We hear much in the pulpit of the insecurity, the vanity and instability of temporal things, but each of us thinks that he will still hold his own. If, however, the insecurity comes " in the form of hussars," this readiness to forsake all turns into curses on the conquerors. We are apparently to think it is positively good if not only our property but also the lives of those dearest to us should be destroyed from time to time by the god-state in order to teach us the vanity of earthly affections. This is one advantage of war. Another is that it inculcates discipline and moral soundness. People who will not endure sovereignty within are brought under the heel of others (pp. 411–13). Kant's proposal of a League of Peace is specifically repudiated. Those know little of the spirit of the people who think that they can make a whole along with others (p. 409) (as e.g. the proud Scot has made with the Englishman), and even if a number of states can make themselves into a family, this union as an individuality would create an opposite and engender an enemy (p. 412). That in all this argument Hegel is in touch with some dismal realities must be admitted. War, like other public calamities, does teach sacrifice to some who did not know it before. It does impose discipline and make democracy difficult. Wider unions are hard to achieve and most easily consolidated by a common enemy. A great humanitarian thinker, like Kant, is not unaware of these grave disharmonies in human life and in the social order. The peculiar vice of Hegel is that to him they are part of the ideal and they receive a non-moral justification from the inhuman conception of the state as a god with a life of its own, reckless of the fibres of human feeling that it rends and mangles to assist its vital processes, devouring its children. Yet the conception of the selfhood of the state is not even carried through with consistency. The state is a self-dependent totality (p. 417), and yet it cannot be an actual individual without relation to other states. The inter-state relations are necessary, therefore, to the existence of each state. As these states are spiritual beings, one would suppose that their relations were of spiritual and, a fortiori, of moral and legal character. Not at all. When we consider their relations their dependence on one another vanishes, and they are put above the moral law. Their relation is other than one of mere morality or private law. Private persons have a court over them. State relations should be of a legal kind (*rechtlich*), but, as there is no power above them to decide what is right, we are here merely in the region of what should be. States may make a stipulation between one another, but at the same time stand above this stipulation, or, as the current phrase goes, their treaties are scraps of paper. As there are no judges, disputes must be decided by war, and the causes of war are quite indeterminate. The state must judge for itself what it will treat as a matter of honour, and is the more inclined to susceptibility (*Rcizbarkeit*) in this respect, the more a strong individuality is driven, through a long internal peace, to seek and procure for itself some matter for activity beyond its bounds (p. 420). Thus there seems no moral limit to the restless ambition of this god. He should in some sense have regard to right in dealing with his fellow-gods, but he may be expected to disregard this recommendation when he is conscious of his own strength, and he need not even wait for any actual injury. The idea of a threatening danger is sufficient. Anticipatory wars are justified (p. 420). Nor is the state to be guided by any philanthropic conception in war. It is to think of its own well-being, the well-being of the state having a quite other justification than that of the individual. It is only the state's concrete existence, not any of the general conceptions that are thought of as moral commands, that can be taken as the principle of its action (p. 421). In only one respect has Hegel failed to anticipate the whole practice of modern Germany, and that is that he lays down that the relations of states remain in war and that in war the possibility of peace is preserved. It is not waged against inner institutions, family and private life. And this is why modern wars are humanely conducted. With this amiable inconsistency, in which Hegel seems to fail to interpret the spirit of his own teaching, we may take leave of the Hegelian state, having seen perhaps enough of it to recognize the germ of the colossal suffering of Europe and of the backward movement that went so far to arrest the civilizing tendencies of the eighteenth and nineteenth centuries.

Dr. Bosanquet follows Hegel in conceiving the state as necessarily one unity among others, a conception which rules out the possibility of a world-state. " We have hitherto (p. 184) spoken of the state and society as almost convertible terms." Having said this, Bosanquet proceeds to a definition of the state. " By the state, then, we mean society as a unit recognized as rightly exercising control over its members through absolute physical power." Questions arise here as to the unit, as to the term " recognize " and as to the term " rightly."

First as to the unit. The limits of this Bosanquet admits " to be determined by what looks like historical accident." But he contends that there is " logic underneath the apparent accident." This so-called logic may be nothing but physical force. What logic incorporated Alsace-Lorraine with Germany ? Bribery incorporated the Irish with the British Parliament. If it is untrue to say with Treitschke that force alone has built up states, it is equally false to shut our eyes to the fact that force has had a great deal to do with the building up of a great many states.

But there is perhaps a more fundamental point. Bosanquet regards the state as necessarily a unit among others (p. 185). " A single independent corporation among other independent corporations." If it is of the essence of the state, as Hegel certainly thought and as Bosanquet seems to think, to be one among many, then society is always something wider than the state. Bosanquet thinks that the area of the state should be as great as is " compatible with the unity of experience which is demanded by effective self-government." In reality there is no such thing as a unity of experience as between the members of a state contrasted with the lack of unity as between members of different states. In the civilized world the ramifications of mutual influence are not bounded by a frontier, but the whole is potentially one society, and for many purposes the relations between corresponding classes of different states are closer than the relations between very different classes within the same state. Instead of defining the state, then, as society, we should speak of it as *a* society, and the difference is much greater than it appears. " A " society is simply a particular organization which may be of great value but which yet might be destroyed and leave society standing. The ultimate obligations of man as a social being are not to any particular society, but to society as such.

Next the state is recognized. We may well ask, By whom? Must it be recognized by all its members? If not recognized as rightly exercising control by some considerable section of its members, does it cease to be a state? And what are the limits, if any, of political obligation in this direction? The question seems unanswerable unless you refer politics back to ethics. A disobedient section will probably put forward certain claims of right which they say that the state that exercises authority over them ignores. If these claims of right are ethically well founded, then their denial of the right of the state to exercise control appears to be justified, and if not, not. So far then from the rights being derivable from the state, the moral authority of the state rests upon the validity of the rights which it asserts.

With this we pass to the third point, of the state as rightly exercising control over its members through absolute physical power. The state has absolute physical power in the sense that it can inflict imprisonment, torture or death if it has an army and a police force, but how far does it do so rightly? Here again we have a question that runs back to ethics. The states in the modern world which claim to be free owe much of their history to the protest of individuals, classes or churches against various applications of physical force which they have denied to be right applications. In a word, Dr. Bosanquet's definition is an intermixture of moral considerations with questions of fact, just those questions which it is the business of philosophy to disentangle.

Dr. Bosanquet goes on to say that every individual must belong to one state and one only because there must be some power which makes the ultimate adjustment of claims. What is the one state to which a Canadian belongs? Is it Canada or is it the British Empire? In all working relations of the Canadian's life it is Canada, and the Canadian law and Canadian custom with which he is in contact. To the non-British world he is simply a British subject and the relations of Canada as a whole are principally, though not wholly, adjusted by the British Empire. It may be said that the British Parliament delegated the bulk of its rights to the Dominion Parliament and can resume them. As a fact it can certainly do nothing of the kind, and the realities of the situation are only expressed by admitting a dual state, a dual loyalty, which under certain circumstances might give rise to sharp conflict. All this is very intelligible if we simply understand the state as an organization coming into being for certain purposes and capable of being adapted, expanded, changed, and even abolished, as may suit those particular purposes. In modern political structure the interweaving of such organizations is playing a growing part. And it is of practical as well as theoretical importance that this growth should not be checked by overdrawn distinctions between what is a state and what is not a state.

The limits of the state which can achieve the kind of individuality required appear to Dr. Bosanquet to admit of simple statement. " The nation-state is the widest organization which has a common experience necessary to found a common life." We have already criticized Dr. Bosanquet's conception of the limitation of common experience to the boundaries of any state short of humanity as a whole. That any philosopher should suggest that the nation-state is the last word in political development is surprising.

In the first place the identity of the nation with the state is perhaps not perfectly realized in any single known political community, while the divergencies in many political communities constitute one of the acute standing problems of most modern states. The only value of the term " nation-state " is that it serves as a mark of distinction on the one hand from the city-state of antiquity and on the other hand of the purely non-national empire, while it further indicates the kind of ideal to which the more fortunate political societies approximate and to which closer approximation is requisite if the problems referred to above are to be solved. These problems, however, are insoluble if the state is the unity on which Bosanquet insists. They are soluble only by recognizing detached allegiances within the state. Austria, for example, solved one of her difficulties fifty years ago by dualism. She may solve her present difficulties by trialism or possibly quadruplism. If her statesmen begin by saying that there must be one Austro-Hungarian state, to which Czech, Slovene, Croat and Serb owe unqualified allegiance, then the future for Austria holds no prospect but the continued menace of warfare.

In the Introduction to his second edition Dr. Bosanquet

seems to have modified his view of the limitation of the state to the boundaries of the nation. " How far even the absolute power of any one group in relation to individuals within it may be interfered with by constitutional tradition or by a conflict of authorities . . . or by international courts or leagues, is a question of degree and detail. . . . There is therefore no technical difficulty in the modification of the nation-state towards larger forms of authoritative co-operation so long as it is made clear to what system of authorities every separate human being is subject in respect to the ultimate adjustment of claims upon him."

Finally, in his recent book *Social and International Ideals*, he carries the subject further by a discussion of the idea of the League of Nations, which has now become a matter of practical politics. Each state, we are now told, is " a member of an ethical family of nations, so far at least as the European world is concerned "—we can hardly suppose Dr. Bosanquet intends to exclude America and other civilized nations—and Mazzini's doctrine is accepted that each state has its individual mission, furnishing its specific contribution to human life. Fundamentally this mission is discharged by the right performance on the part of each state of its internal function, the maintenance of the conditions of a good life, and an entire chapter is given to the development of the thesis that, if each state would look at home and reform itself, there would be no conflict of states and no wars. As a remedy for war, this is a little like the proposal that each man should reform himself as a remedy for social injustice. It is quite true that, if every one would reform himself, injustices would disappear, and similarly, if every state would reform itself, conflicts of states would disappear, but what is to happen if one or two or three states cultivate their own gardens, while other states cast covetous eyes on these gardens ? That is the question which exercises the supporters of the League of Nations, who find in the requirement for internal reform nothing but a pious platitude as long as security against external disturbance is not guaranteed.

Dr. Bosanquet contends that beyond the state " there is no organized moral world," and that an organized moral world involves a unity which must grow out of a pervading will.[1] The advocate of the League of Nations will reply that he is seeking to establish an organized moral world, such as may give expression to the pervading desire for peace. Dr. Bosanquet answers[2] that " though you may find several communities desiring peace and though they make a league to enforce it, their general wills taken together are not one will ; that is, they have not in common the same object or views of life." It will be found that the real bond in a league of communities will be the bond of force. There will be a solid foundation for international unity only if there is a prevailing general will. This cannot be effected by setting up a machinery. The machinery must be a consequence, not the cause. Whether a true general will can in fact be realized in an area " exceeding what has generally been called the territories of a nation " is a problem for the future. The essential thing for the present is to insist that " the foundation of all sound political thinking is the supremacy of absolute values in the self-moulded life of the community."

The entire argument rests at bottom on an assertion of distinction in kind where there is only distinction of degree. The unity of the will in the state, except as an expression of a partial agreement for certain purposes, is, as we have seen, a fiction. The state itself frequently transcends what has been usually called the territories of a nation. The British Empire consists of many nations and many dependencies, but it has been shown to act together for certain purposes with great effect. Should it seek to unify itself for other purposes, it would be wrecked. Why cannot all civilized humanity then unite itself for some purposes and not others ? Such a union, for Dr. Bosanquet, is mere machinery. We may agree that without a will to back it, the machinery would be unavailing. But Dr. Bosanquet himself admits the

[1] P. 313.   [2] P. 314.

converse proposition that the will would be unavailing without the machinery. What are those to do who have the will and. desire to cultivate it ? What can they do but endeavour to persuade others to agree with them in setting up the institutions required to express that will ? If they get their way, the will has won its first victory. It has so far established itself, and that is the first step to consolidation. The machinery, Dr. Bosanquet objects, involves force, but the state itself involves force. In the procedure of the state we do not wait until every one agrees. We win enough agreement to make possible the application of force to the remainder who differ.

Dr. Bosanquet's discussion brings out the contrast between the metaphysical way of regarding social problems and the way which is at once ethical and scientific, or, in a word, practical. The metaphysical method says that in the state there is a real self and beyond it there are only external and mechanical relations. The practical spirit says men are involved in innumerable relations with their fellows, which require organization because, if unorganized, they are left to anarchy and disaster. All sorts of different organizations are required to deal with the different relations of men. They must be united for some purposes and left free for others. One sphere of life may be controlled by one organization and another by another, and both organizations may in turn be brought as parts within some common organization for certain purposes. Where there is to be unity and where there is to be freedom, what purposes are to be assigned to one organization and what to another, these are questions to be determined with such wisdom and foresight as we can win from experience in practical affairs. The utmost plasticity is required in adapting the form of organization to the multiplicity of human requirements. What ruins everything is the conception of an absolute sovereignty that admits no independent rights, an absolute unity that leaves no room for divergence, an absolute demarcation between a state which claims the entire devotion of its citizens and all other political or social organizations which are conceived as mechanical, arbitrary and insignificant.

At the conclusion of his earlier work,[1] Dr. Bosanquet passes to the question of the morality of state action. The discussion is inconclusive and so involved that it is difficult to grasp the real upshot. He seems to have great difficulty in admitting that the state can act immorally, but not wholly to repudiate its possibility. When he draws a distinction between the state and its agents, he seems to open the door to very Jesuitical interpretations. First he asks the question, When an act is immoral, can the state as such really have willed it ? He waives this, however, as a mere refinement, so that one does not like to press the point against him personally. But it must be remarked that for the state as one organization of human beings to will something unjust to another organization of human beings seems no more difficult than for a family to act under an impulse of collective selfishness for its own good against the rights of another family, or for a Trade Union to inflict unjustifiable injury on another Trade Union. It is merely the confusion of the state as an organization with the rational will which causes any difficulty in the matter.

Bosanquet finds it hard to see how the state can commit theft or murder. History has not found it difficult to conceive governments and statesmen committing theft of other people's territories, and when Bosanquet denies (on p. 338) that a country is guilty of murder when it carries on war, he overlooks the justice or injustice of that war. Is it not in all seriousness collective murder on a large scale to carry war into the bounds of another country without a justification which must not only satisfy the state that plans the war but an impartial tribunal ? Between an unjustifiable war and an act of brigandage there is no moral difference. The difficulty is to fix the guilt of individuals, but this is because the responsibility is diffused. It would generally speaking be harsh to charge the citizen soldier, acting partly under compulsion,

[1] P. 322.

partly from a sense of loyalty, with bloodguiltiness ; and yet the finer minds would, and do, refuse to fight in a quarrel which they are convinced is unjust. The *Biglow Papers* contain a sounder morality than Bosanquet's—

> " Ef you take a sword an' dror it,
>   Go an' stick a feller thru,
>   Guv'ment aint to answer for it,
>   God'll send the bill to you."

But the responsibility of statesmen is surely much more direct, and those who are actively responsible for bringing on a war cannot as individuals shift the moral burden from their own consciences. If a higher international morality is to be achieved, it is precisely by reversing the argument of the idealist. The individual must not be able to shelter himself from moral responsibility behind the state. But the actions of the state being judged on the same principle as those of individuals, every individual supporting the state in its action must be rightly regarded as assuming a personal responsibility in so doing. As to the state itself, it may be said that an intangible thing like an organization cannot be the subject of moral guilt. Nevertheless that organization may be condemned as a bad organization and it may justly suffer punishments in the infliction of losses or penalties.

By a curiously involved argument the private honour of the agents of the state is distinguished from the good faith of the state itself. Dr. Bosanquet argues, so far justly, that the state is not to be blamed for the ill-faith or other misdeed of its agents. That is of course true on condition that the state does not consciously benefit by this misdeed. So much Bosanquet seems to admit, but he goes on to say that the agent is likely to go wrong if he mixes up the obligations of the state with his private honour. Precisely the contrary view must be maintained. If the agent of the state enters into an undertaking which, as an honourable man, he would not do on his own account, he is doing wrong and no reason of state justifies him. So low is the reputation of states that, for example, it was

palpable that the personal respect for Sir Edward Grey's
character was a greater asset to British diplomacy in the
years before the war and in the events leading up to it
than any word of any government as government. The
private standard is above the public standard, and therefore
it is by insisting rather that statesmen are bound to act
as honourable men than that honourable men should act
as servants of the state that we can best hope to raise
the moral level of the state.

The cause of all the hesitancy with which Bosanquet
deals with this question is to be found in a paragraph on
pp. 324-5. The state, we learn here, " has no determinate
function in a larger community, but is itself the supreme
community ; the guardian of a whole world, but not a
factor within an organized moral world. The moral
relations presuppose an organized life ; but such a life is
only within the state and not in the relations between the
state and other communities." The smaller part of the
profound error found in this passage is the mistake as to
fact. Organized relations of many kinds do exist at
present outside the boundaries of the state, commercial
relations, religious relations, the more ideal relations of
community of thought, literature, art and the rest. But
the fundamental fallacy is the conception that morality
depends upon the legal organization which is the distinctive
mark of the state. Moral relations exist as between all
human beings, if not between all living beings, that come
into any sort of contact with one another. For their full
and adequate expression these relations no doubt require
an organized expression. If, where they are close and
frequent, they fail to obtain such organized expression,
there is danger of moral anarchy. This is exactly the
position which has arisen among nations of the present
day. Here we have relations becoming ever closer and
more vital, but a failure in the attempt to build up
institutions to express, to shield and to develop the moral
requirements which those relations impose. The vice of
the idealist theory of the state is that it denies the need
and even the possibility of such transcendence of state

limits. This theory, true to its fundamental misconception that the ideal is inherent in the nature of the existing order, proceeds to justify and apply the fallacy. There is no more glaring instance of that fallacy of philosophic idealism which has been expressed by saying that instead of seeking to realize the ideal it idealizes the real.

In his new volume Dr. Bosanquet discusses the question anew and repudiates with some warmth the accusation of denying the moral responsibility of the state. One is glad to think this was never his intention, but in view of the character noted above of his earlier discussion, it is not surprising if he laid himself open to some misunderstanding. He now asks his critics: [1] " Is our fault in saying that the community, which asserts itself through the state, *is* a moral being and *has* a conscience, or is not a moral being and has not a conscience ? They seem to me in effect to say both at once, but only one can be true." The reply to this is that Dr. Bosanquet has appeared to his critics to say both at once, that he has greatly exaggerated the moral character of the state in certain relations and appeared to depreciate it as unduly in others. This double and opposite exaggeration still, I feel, subsists in his new statement. The moral character of the state is exaggerated to the point of caricature when it is spoken of as " sole organizer of rights and as guardian of moral values." On the other hand, it is depreciated unduly in its external relations. Dr. Bosanquet repeats the allegation that there exists no organized moral world, prescribing the course of duty to the state. It is not the mere absence of sanction that makes the difference between the state and the individual ; it is more—" the absence of a recognized moral order such as to guide the conscience itself."

On this I have two comments to make. In the first place, if the state is the conscience of mankind, the sole guardian of rights and duties, the moral individual in a much more real sense than the simple man or woman, how comes it that it has built up no moral order in its external relations? Here are states (Dr. Bosanquet must in this relation admit the plural) in constant intercourse with each other. Each of them is a moral being with a conscience much more highly developed than that of any individual, yet on his showing these gifted beings have built up no recognized order to guide their consciences. They are left to anarchy and to do what is right in their own eyes, for this is what it comes to when it is said that the state must see in the moral world of which it is the guardian, the only definite guide in any difficult problem of its relations to others. It is a paradox that verges on contradiction that highly moral beings in close relations to one another should evolve no moral order and no common understanding.

Secondly, Dr. Bosanquet depreciates unduly the partial moral order which has actually been established. I do not recollect to have come across the phrase " international law " in the course of his discussion, nor in fact do I see it in the index. There is a law as between states and there has been " *Sittlichkeit* " between them, very imperfect no doubt, yet not without its value. What has paralysed the development of international law and morality is, on the side of theory, just that doctrine of state absolutism of which the idealistic theory of the state is the most subtle justification. Every organization of men tends to become conscienceless because it forms an internal public opinion wherein men back one another in the pursuit of everything that tends to the interest or feeds the pride in which, as members of the organization, they share. But in so great an organization as the state the impartial opinion of outsiders scarcely makes itself heard and every plea for right or reasonableness is denounced as treacherous. It is the high duty of philosophy to look beyond this narrow standpoint and seek the universal view. When philosophy deserts its duty, who will fulfil it ? International anarchy is not due to philosophy but to the passions of men, but the restraint which humanitarian philosophy has sought to impose has been fatally loosened by the sophistications of idealism.

8

Developing his position in his recent volume, Dr. Bosanquet finds a double difficulty in the conception of " an organism of humanity " which he admits to be the natural extension of the idea of the social organism. The difficulty is (*a*) that humanity in fact possesses no communal consciousness whatever. Neither did England under the Heptarchy, nor France under the Merovingians. A common consciousness is a thing which grows, and Dr. Bosanquet admits that the defect might be overcome. The idea of humanity is due in part to the Stoic philosophy and in part to the great world religions, and if it has never fully matured, neither has it ever perished. It has never lost its appeal to the greater and deeper thinkers and teachers and it has continually inspired the missionary effort of the church. The conditions of an effective unity of mankind to-day are at least as matured as the conditions of an effective German unity in the eighteenth century, or an effective French unity during the Hundred Years' War. And just as a farsighted and wide-minded Frenchman or German was he who realized the unity underlying differences and prepared the way for its growth, so the farsighted man of to-day is he who holds to the unity of human nature and the common interests of mankind and places them above all causes of quarrel. But (*b*) Dr. Bosanquet finds no adequate expression of the higher human qualities in the aggregate of human beings. The valuable things are the possessions of particular communities and, " to put it bluntly, a duty to realize the best life cannot be shown to coincide with the duty to the masses of mankind." We do not need to be told that the achievements of ancient Athens and modern France are not shared by Hottentots and Kaffirs. But it does not follow that Hottentots and Kaffirs are outside the pale of rights and duties, and I do not suppose Dr. Bosanquet would contend that they are. But to say this is to admit the fundamental principle of universalism, that all human beings, as human, are within the scope of the fundamental moral law. Special obligations arise in distinct communities, but these are developments of common obligations which man owes to man. To make them override these fundamentals, to push devotion to a group to the point at which it breaks with the common rule, is the sin of all group morality, of which the Machiavellian doctrine of the state is the standing example.

Finally, Dr. Bosanquet imputes to the Comtists the mistake of identifying humanity as a real corporate being with the aggregate of human beings. That this is a complete misapprehension will be shown by the following passage by a distinguished Comtist :

" No one thinks that when he mentions the word England or France or Germany, he is talking of a ghost or a phantom. Nor does he mean a vast collection of so many millions of men in the abstract ; so many million ghosts. Man in the abstract is of all abstractions the most unreal. By England we mean the prejudices, customs, traditions, history, peculiar to Englishmen, summed up in the present generation, in the living representatives of the past history. So with Humanity. . . . Is such a religion self-worship ? . . . What explains the error is the belief that by Humanity we mean the same thing as the human race. We mean something widely different. Of each man's life, one part has been personal, the other social : one part consists in actions for the common good, the other part in actions of pure self-indulgence, and even of active hostility to the common welfare. Such actions retard the progress of Humanity, though they cannot arrest it : they disappear, perish, and are finally forgotten. There are lives wholly made up of actions such as these. They form no part of Humanity. Humanity consists only of such lives, and only of those parts of each man's life, which are impersonal, which are social, which have converged to the common good." [1]

The " Comtist " Humanity is mankind in so far as it forms a spiritual unity. To this unity individuals, races, communities contribute, some more and some less, some perhaps not at all ; and the contribution may be conscious or unconscious. Dr. Bosanquet should find no difficulty here. The state is for him a real corporate being which has an aggregate of citizens for its members, some of whom contribute to its unity much, some little, and others, as individuals, perhaps not at all, while the contribution

[1] J. H. Bridges, *Essays and Addresses*, pp. 86-8.

may in any case be conscious or unconscious. There are difficulties in the Comtist conception, but it is both more spiritual and truer to fact than the idealistic conception. More spiritual because it goes below the externals of unity and relies on the permanence and penetrativeness of the inward forces which, uniting man to man, have built up the fabric of collective achievement. It is, so to say, a unity of the church rather than of the state. More true to fact because it recognizes that the higher values, on which Dr. Bosanquet insists, are not the achievements of one state or one nation, but of many, that the history of thought, ethics, religion or art, is not a history of separate communities but a world history. The co-operation, conscious or unconscious, which has wrought the best things in civilized life, is one to which races and peoples have contributed unequally, and some have not contributed at all, but it is one which far transcends the limit of any people or nation, not to speak of any state.

But below the idea of humanity, which he deems merely a confusion, Dr. Bosanquet detects a darker and more dangerous aspiration. He " suspects " current ideas of the international future to be seriously affected by popular notions of progress and an evanescence of evil, which should " compensate for the wrongs and sufferings of the past." To the idealist this is sheer blasphemy against the Absolute Dr. Bosanquet tells us that he personally believes in a nobler future, but since the Absolute is perfection and since evil exists, evil is necessary to perfection and its evanescence seems " altogether contradictory." Its disappearance is certainly a remote danger. The world need not be under the apprehension of a premature drying up of the springs of misery and wrong. In the meanwhile it is instructive to find that in the last resort the gospel of state absolutism and opposition to the League of Nations rests on the necessity of evil as a part of the permanent scheme of things. Dr. Bosanquet may say that at any rate future good is no compensation for past wrong. In a sense, we must all agree, wrong done cannot be undone. Blighted and ruined lives cannot be lived anew. Yet, if it is a question of the depth and genuineness of the feeling that a better future for the world is worth the sacrifice of the present generation, the idealist may bethink himself of many a young man, German as well as English, who has found in this thought an alleviation of the stark horrors of the trenches and the near approach of mutilation or death. It is not a question of compensation, but of the final meaning of the painful struggle of human life. If the world cannot be made incomparably better than it has hitherto been, then the struggle has no issue, and we had better strengthen the doctrine of the militant state and arm it with enough high explosive to bring life to an end. At any rate the final question is laid bare. There are those who believe life can be made good. There are those who believe it is good enough already. There are those who see life as an effort towards a harmony, of which as yet we see only the germs. They are well aware of all the tragedy that is involved in growth and do not delude themselves with any dream of personal reparation, but they recognize in the evolutionary process a principle which is neither the blind whirl of conflicting passions nor the clash of egoisms, but the emergence of a spirit of harmonious freedom, and on this they rest, and with this they identify themselves. There are those again for whom the world as it is is the incarnation of the ideal, for whom change is secondary and of no vital significance. For them evil must be justified as essential to good, though a more self-contradictory conception than that of good maintaining evil for its own purposes cannot well be devised. To the former the turning-point in the development of harmony is the clear consciousness and the adequate expression of the unity of mankind. To the latter it is a source of apprehension because it would cut the tap-root of those egoisms of state and nation, class and sex, colour and race, which engender the massive miseries of the world.

We have summed up the metaphysical theory in three propositions. (1) The individual attains his true self and freedom in conformity to his real will ; (2) this real will is the general will ; and (3) the general will is embodied in the state. We have seen reasons for denying all these propositions. We have maintained that there is no distinction between the real will and the actual will, that the will of the individual is not identical with the general will and that the rational order, which the general will is supposed to maintain, is not confined and may be opposed to the state organization. We have suggested that serious fallacies, as calamitous morally as they are logically vicious, are involved in the political philosophy which turns upon this conception. But it would be unfair to the metaphysical theory of the state to leave the impression that it has always received the kind of interpretation which we have here examined. In the hands of Green, for example, the notion of the general will is stated in terms which bring it into closer relation to the facts of experience, and the relation of the state to the individual is so defined as to approach far more closely to the organic conception of society. It is not my purpose here either to explain or criticize Green's *Principles of Political Obligation*, a work of great power and of some weaknesses, which could not be adequately examined in anything short of an independent treatise, but for the sake of fairness to Green and to living writers who have drawn their principal inspiration from him rather than Hegel, I would call attention to one or two points in which Green departs notably from the Hegelian model.

First and above all, the right of the individual runs through Green's entire argument. For Green, each man has to attain his own good, realize his own perfection as an integral part of the common good. If society has a claim upon him for the performance of his duty, he likewise has a claim upon society for the power to fulfil it. (P. 347:) "The claim or right of the individual to have certain powers secured to him by society, and the counterclaim of society to exercise certain powers over the individual, alike rest on the fact that these powers are necessary to the fulfilment of man's vocation as a moral being, to an effectual self-devotion to the work of developing the perfect character in himself and others." The state does not absorb the individual. It is (p. 443) "a body of persons, recognized by each other as having rights and possessing certain institutions for the maintenance of those rights." The reciprocal relations of state and society could not be put better in a single and succinct phrase. The rights of the individual certainly do not exist independently of society, but they are conditions of its own best life and therefore of the best life of the individuals which constitute it, which society is bound to recognize. (P. 351:) "Only through the possession of rights can the power of the individual freely to make a common good his own have reality given to it. Rights are what may be called the negative realization of this power. That is, they realize it in the sense of providing for its free exercise, of securing the treatment of one man by another as equally free with himself ; but they do not realize it positively, because their possession does not imply that in any active way the individual makes a common good of his own. The possession of them, however, is the condition of this positive realization of the moral capacity, and they ought to be possessed because this end (in the sense explained) ought to be attained."

Where Green is less happy, as I think, is in his discussion of the rights which society ought to recognize but does not. Thus he tells us on p. 416 "a right against society, in distinction from a right to be treated as a member of society, is a contradiction in terms." The truth which this sentence contains is that a right is a social relation just as much as a duty is a social relation, your right being something which I or some one else or society at large owes to you. But Green is apt to confuse the social character of rights with the recognition of rights, even going so far as to say (p. 446) "rights are made by recognition. There is no right 'but thinking makes it so.'" This is not consistent with his admission (p. 351) of "rights which remain rights though any particular state or all states refuse to recognize them " ; a sense in which he has justly said a slave has natural rights. He gives the truth in the following sentence (p. 450) : " They are ' natural ' in the sense of being independent of, and in conflict with, the laws of the state in which he lives, but they are not independent of social relations." What is needed to make these positions consistent is merely to observe that social relations are not all conscious relations. The position is well stated in an early lecture (p. 353) : " The capacity, then, on the part of the individual of conceiving a good as the same for himself and others, and of being determined to action by that conception, is the foundation of rights ; and rights are the condition of that capacity being realized." Such a condition is something objective, independent of recognition. If any one can prove that some specific condition is in fact requisite to the realization of a good life, then that condition is scientifically demonstrated to be a right, though it may never have been recognized from the beginning of time to the present day, and though society may refuse to recognize it now. It is in this sense that all true rights are natural rights.

In all this discussion Green is on the track of the truth, but is obstructed by his idealistic presupposition that what is real must somehow be in the minds of men. Enough, however, has been said to show that Green's conception of the common good, far from overriding the individual, assumes his participation as an individual, and, far from ignoring his rights, jealously preserves them as conditions under which he is a free and rational being to achieve a good which is his own as well as the good of society.[1]

---

[1] In his new volume, *Social and International Ideals*, Dr. Bosanquet advances a fresh definition of the state, which is more in line with Green's way of thinking. " I understand by the state the power which, as an organ of the community, has the function of maintaining the external conditions necessary to the best life. These conditions are called rights. They are the claims recognized by the whole of the community as the *sine quâ non* of the highest obtainable fulfilment of the capacities for the best life possessed by its best members." This seems to carry a much fuller recognition of the individual than is usual in Dr. Bosanquet's writings. If

Nor does the general will in Green figure as the common self. It is rather an element in popular psychology, which Green finds in experience. Thus he speaks (p. 404) of " that impalpable congeries of the hopes and fears of a people, bound together by common interests and sympathy, which we call the general will." For Green it is the common will and reason of men, that is " the will and reason of men as determined by social relations, as interested in each other, as acting together for common ends." In these expressions we are at any rate in contact with reality. It may be said that they are vague, but Green might reply that so also are the facts which he is describing. That is to say, the actual extent to which men are swayed by common interests, the degree of their allegiance to the social order, the strength of the emotion prompting to obedience or warring against it are not rigidly determined, they fluctuate from people to people, even from district to district and from occasion to occasion. There is, he seems to say, a common good, which to the reflective mind is a definite conception and a clear ideal, but which is vaguely and partially apprehended by the ordinary man, so that it is rather the diffused sense of the common good than a clear purpose of realizing it which operates as a force in the ordinary life of society. These are propositions, I would suggest, rather in social psychology than in metaphysics.

When Green goes on to contend that will, in the sense which he has described, and not force is the basis of the state, it becomes clear that his conception of the state has to be shaped to suit his definition. But of course he admits the element of force and shows how it is fused with moral factors and in the end saves his general proposition by excluding political organizations based on power. (P. 443:) " We only count Russia a state by a sort of

consistently pressed, it would, I think, lead to the reconstruction of his entire theory, but the chapter from which it is taken is professedly not a correction but a restatement of his theory of the state, and the criticisms on this theory in general must therefore stand unaffected.

courtesy on the supposition that the power of the Czar, though subject to no constitutional control, is so far exercised in accordance with a recognized tradition of what the public good requires as to be on the whole a sustainer of rights."

Green's principle, therefore, is less paradoxical, perhaps also less important, than appears at first sight. If will not force is the basis of the state, that is because only that society is a state which is based not on force but on will. It would be unfair, however, to reduce Green's argument to a truism. We may fairly put his conclusion in this form. In every organized society there are other elements than force sustaining the general conformity to law, and in the higher organization of society conditions are realized in which force recedes further and further into the background, goodwill at each step taking its place. Only societies which have made some sensible progress in this direction deserve the name of states. This definition would seem to be justified by the comparative study of political institutions.

Enough has perhaps been said to show that in Green's hands the conception of the general will is not allowed to overwhelm the individual, nor to override the moral law, but that the state is thought of rather as a guarantor to the individual of the conditions which enable him to fulfil his functions as a moral being. It may be objected that if we go behind Green's philosophy to his metaphysics, we shall find ourselves involved in the old difficulties of the universal and the particular and once more find personality absorbed in the universal self. This may be true, but it is a criticism of Green as a metaphysician rather than of Green as a political thinker. His living interest was in practical life, the strength of his grasp lay upon the hard problems of social reform. He was at his best in working through practical issues to the principles guiding them. As he receded from these principles to the ultimate theory of ethics and metaphysics, his grasp grew weaker and his meaning is often lost in obscurity and confusion. Descending again from this misty region to the living world, we find the man for whom principles at least mean something which will affect the life of human beings, which will guide them in wisdom or mislead them in folly, will teach them to ensue the happiness of their kind or justify them in their pride and ambition, which are the cause of misery in society. In his political lectures Green never forgets that theoretical principles are charged with weighty meaning for the lives of men.

If we compare Green's account of the general will with that of Bosanquet and others, we shall, I think, arrive at the conclusion that several distinct conceptions are covered by this term which must be held apart if any such phrases are to be used at all without breeding confusion. (1) In the first place there is a conception of the common good, whether real or supposed. The common good is not the same thing as the common will, though if there were such a thing as a common will, it is presumably the common good at which it would aim. The common good is the well-being actually shared by .the members of society, or conceived as desirable for the members of society, either, therefore, something actually existent or something which may be brought about. It may be regarded as realized or realizable in certain permanent institutions and conditions of life. (2) We may distinguish such permanent conditions from a particular object which may be conceived as a part of the common good for the time being, e.g. victory in war. This we may call a common aim. (3) Corresponding to the common good or the common aim there may be a will to maintain the common good or to achieve the common aim. This may be called the good will.[1] It may exist in any individual, but, as existing in a single individual, it would not seem appropriate to speak of it as a general will. It is just the will of a particular man to secure a common good or a common purpose. (4) But, further,. such a will may be diffused more or less widely in society. If the will of a society were so united that every one of its members willed one and the same

[1] Good at least from the point of view of the society. One might call it the loyal will.

common object, as e.g. if the whole society is bent upon victory in a war, there would be something which we could appropriately and unambiguously describe as a general will, that is to say, a will active in all the members of a society as individuals to achieve an object by their organized efforts for their society as a whole. (5) If, further, we suppose all the members of a society to understand and appreciate the permanent good of the society as a whole and to will the necessary means for securing it, there would similarly be a general will to promote the common good. We may allow a little further latitude, and if such a will is shared, not by the whole of society but by a majority, we may still call it a general will, but for this particular case no special term really seems requisite. The general will here is simply the will of the majority. (6) But this is not the sense of the general will which seems really to be intended by the phrase. To interpret Green's expressions we must think rather of a network of psychological forces making on the whole in a determinate direction, generally speaking for the maintenance of a certain social structure, and more specifically for the attainment of certain definite objects. This network of forces will in a free society obtain expression ultimately in the will of the majority, but it is a good deal more complex and subtle than the content of any majority vote on a specific issue. What goes to make up the bent of the public mind in this sense is not merely so many definite acts of will in such and such a number of individuals. It is the intense conviction in some, the relative feebleness in others, the tacit acquiescence in one man, the partisan feeling in another, the support of a certain section on one particular part of the issue in spite of indifference or hostility on other portions of the issue, a prejudice which buttresses up the case on this side, a weakness which paralyses opposition on another side—a miscellaneous congeries of impulses driven hither and thither, out of all of which there will emerge through reams of controversy some tangible result. Will, which means the basis of clearly thought out action, is really a bad expression

for this unorganized mass of psychological forces of every
sort and kind that actually go to the making up of great
political decisions. It will probably be true, with Green,
to hold that within this congeries there is a permanent
element partly above and partly below the level of consciousness, guided directly or indirectly by considerations
bearing on the common good. There are, for example,
people who will not put themselves about much for justice
in general but will be shocked by some act of concrete
iniquity with which they come into personal contact.
Those who have not been troubled to oppose a bad law in
principle find themselves irked by one of its applications.
Conversely, the normal man who does not generalize about
the social good will deal with practical issues often enough
in the way which principle would require. (7) And
lastly, though we have taken exception to the description
of the social tradition as an embodiment of the objective reason, we have not of course denied that thought
and will have gone to the building up of institutions. It
is not, as we have repeatedly maintained, one thought
and one will, but the combination of many minds thinking
and willing, each by its own lights and each acting too
often in accordance with its selfish interests. None the
less there is a sense in which the institutions and traditions
of society imply a certain social mentality. The acceptance of such traditions, though generally unreflective,
cannot be wholly unconscious, and each individual as he
accepts them fits himself into a scheme of life, not as
voluntarily choosing that scheme as a whole, but as
accepting his part in it. This acceptance affects the
mind of each individual, calling forth one faculty and
repressing another, and so modifies the mental growth.
Thus the outer behaviour of society as seen in its manners
and customs must have an inner mentality to match.
So far as there is discrepancy a change will take place in
institutions. To express this aspect of social life, we might
speak of social mentality, provided we understand that
the kind of unity which the term expresses is not the
unity of a person or self but that of many centres of
thought and will in interaction.

One or another of these meanings seem to be in the mind of those who use the term "general will"; but the real objection to the term is that in so far as it is will it is not general, and in so far as it is general it is not will. The common good is explicitly willed by a minority of thinking and public-spirited individuals. What is general is more undefined and perhaps indefinable, a participation in the variegated mass of psychological forces out of which the actions and development of the community emerge.

We may be asked in conclusion whether after all we are to entirely deny any further meaning and reality to the general will. Was it not admitted at the beginning that there is a sense in which society is more than its members, and is it not this sense which the general will expresses? We can understand the service of our country. Can we in the same way appreciate the service to an indefinite number of individuals like ourselves, and is that what we rely upon in patriotism or in other forms of social duty? Is the collective life of society to go for nothing, and can it all be resolved away into its constituent atoms?

The broad answer to this question can, I think, only be found in the qualifications which we introduced to the statement that the life of a whole is more than that of its parts. The proposition is true, as we saw, only in this sense : that the life of the whole is more or other than that of the parts as they exist or would exist outside the whole. The body is something other than the cells which compose it, for this simple reason among others, that the cells die when separated from the body and therefore rapidly cease to be that which they at present are. But that the body is other than the totality of the cells composing it as they exist within the body, as they function in unison with one another, is a different and, as I think, an untrue proposition. We move in this region between two poles of fallacy. Wherever we have a whole consisting of parts, we are tempted to say that the whole is something other than the sum of its parts, whereby our view of the parts is distorted and the effect of their interactions ignored.

Or, in reaction from this view, we are tempted to say the parts alone are real and that the whole is only a way of regarding them or at best a superficial consequence of their juxtaposition in certain relations to one another. Both these theories are untrue. The first theory always and the second of those wholes which have any distinctive character of their own.

If I cast my eye idly over the leaves strewn on the lawn, I may count them and discover that there are thirty-seven, and treat the thirty-seven as forming a whole. This numerical whole is nothing to the actual leaves. As I count, three of the thirty-seven have run away with the wind and instead of thirty-seven I have thirty-four, which not having been moved are just what they were before. Such a numerical whole is the limiting case in which the parts are unaffected by the totality. It is just their arithmetical sum, no more and no less. If I gather the leaves into a heap, they are at least an aggregate that can be picked up and carried away. But still the aggregate has no permanence and its effect upon the parts is very small and very casual. Unless they happen to be somewhat crushed out of shape by pressure, the leaves will experience no change in passing into the whole and out of it again. If, on the other hand, I consider the leaf itself, even the dead leaf, it is something more than an aggregate. It consists of parts no doubt; but the parts are connected by definite ties. The leaf acts as a whole. If the wind catches a part of it, that part carries the rest along with it. Such a whole of parts in a determinate arrangement which for some purpose act together, is a structure which is in every respect as real and significant as the elements which compose it. What we call the onesided analytic tendency is the tendency to deny this, to think the cells something more real than the leaf, which is thus conceived only as a certain arrangement of cells, and the molecules of protoplasm more real than the cells and the atoms more real than the molecule. We get rid of a bunch of fallacies incidental to this line of argument when we refuse to speak of more or less real altogether.

Atoms, molecules, protoplasm, cells, leaf, all are just real or unreal. What we can say is that in many cases the elements are more permanent than the whole which they constitute. Certain physical molecules, for example, remain, I suppose, when the dead leaf begins to decompose, and it is this permanence, or supposed permanence, of the simple elements underlying complex structures, which has given the illusion of their greater reality. Conversely, in many cases the whole is more permanent than the parts. E.g. the living organism is always absorbing and excreting material elements. It remains while its components change. The components do not indeed pass out of existence when they leave the whole, but in proportion as the structure is organic they are profoundly modified. The cell does not survive the leaf, nor does the protoplasm, as protoplasm, the cell. Of any organic structure this principle will hold true. The parts will not survive the structure unaltered. Something in each may survive, but it will not be exactly that which existed within the whole.

Now in human society, as in the material world, there are many fortuitous aggregations, producing slight contact between individuals. The people who happen to be walking along a street at a particular time may be numerically conceived of as a whole, though they are barely modified by any contact with one another. A crowd is more united than this, though it has no structure, but for the time being people are affected by close contact with one another, and to that extent even a crowd is a unity and a reality, though not one with endurance. Passing on, we find all sorts of associations into which men can enter, affecting their lives in very varying degrees. When the effect is slight, we may well say that it is the individuals that are permanent, and if the society is broken up, it is just resolved into its component individuals, who remain very much what they were before. When we come to the deeper and more stable associations, this would no longer be true. The life of the family is an integral part of the men and women that compose it. When it breaks up the lives of those that remain may be tragically altered ;

certainly they are very different from what they would have been if they had never known a family life. The same thing would be true of a religious body, or of a state, or of any great movement, intellectual, social or political, into which a man throws himself. All these deeper associations are of the organic type. They express important elements, perhaps fundamental elements, in the lives which compose them, so that without them those individuals would be essentially other than they are.

If thus for a moment we think of the life or value of such an association in terms of individuals, we must in turn think of the individuals as contributing and consciously contributing to the life of the whole. If the soldier is told that to die for England means to die for English men and women, he might say that that was good enough for him, but he might also go on to say that it is not merely for men and women as men and women, but for men and women as continuing to lead a certain life, as maintaining and developing the tradition which is essentially England. This tradition lives in nothing but individuals; all of it that is incorporated in material, even the land itself, however much that is the object of affection, vanishes into insignificance apart from the humanity which it subserves. The tradition, on the other hand, might flourish as well on foreign soil, as colonization proves, and as was understood by William the Silent when he thought of transporting the entire population of Holland and Zeeland to a part of the world where they could maintain their life free from the empire-state which was crushing it.

Thus the character of a social whole is as much in danger of being misunderstood when it is resolved into its component individuals as it is when conceived as separate from them, as though it were not made by them. The true organic theory is that the whole is just what is constituted by the co-operation of the parts, neither more nor less, not more real nor less real, not of higher nor of inferior value. In saying this we must take time into account. All the parts strictly means all that have been or will be while the whole endures. When this succession of members is taken into account, it is true to equate the perfectly organic whole with the sum of its parts in their co-operative activity. But there is a sense in which a whole may be less, and a sense in which it may be more than its existing parts. (1) Wholes in general, even relatively organic wholes, may engage only a portion of the activity or capacity of their members. This is eminently true of human associations, none of which embrace the entire life of man. In such a case it is only the portion incurred in the whole that can be said to live or die with the whole, and only so far as that portion is concerned that there is anything of the nature of an organic union. One of the fallacies of the metaphysical theory is to identify the individual with one particular association, and to speak of his obligations to that association in terms only applicable to the sum of his duties and interests in all the relations of his life. (2) While some wholes are less, others, and particularly those which engage the deeper nature of men, are more permanent than their members. When we go, for example, below the state to the nation and beyond the nation to the great movements of civilization, we come to things in which the whole truly is something far greater than any of the parts that constitute it at any one moment. What concerns humanity is that such wholes should be maintained in so far as they serve its abiding interest. But this again is not, if we think it out, to erect the whole into an object distinct and opposed to those who have been, are or will be its members. It is merely to grasp its far-reaching extension, its deeply rooted continuity. The nation is all the generations which compose it as long as they maintain a certain unity and as long as the thread of causation remains uncut. More than this it is not.[1]

[1] When taken as more it will be found to be really less. If the good of the state is opposed to that of its component members, it is because its good is being found in ends which do not make life really better, for example, glory, wealth, expansion and power. Such ends the masses may serve in their capacity of " cannon-

In what terms we are to describe the reality of the social wholes is a standing difficulty of sociology. They are, as we have seen, of organic character, yet, if we speak of them as organisms, we are liable to confound them with animals or plants, which they are not. Essentially they are unities of mind. Their component elements are minds and the relations into which these elements enter are determined by mental operations. Yet if we speak of them as personalities, we are liable to the fallacy of the common self. Social inquiry suffers from nothing so much as a lack of technical terms or of suitable metaphor to supply the place of technical terms. It has to use words derived from other orders of experience and conceptions elaborated in other sciences. What we must most eschew is any term suggesting a form of unity realized in some other whole than the particular social whole which we are consider-

---

fodder," but then they are not parts of the state but mere living tools, the effective organization consisting of the rulers and generals who want the glory. At bottom, when any organized human society is alleged to have a good other than that of its members, it means a good, at least a supposed good, of some of its members without regard to the remainder. It may be said that these unhappy ones acquiesce, e.g. when the multitude lets itself be dominated by its chiefs and led by them to the slaughter in the desire to share even in a subordinate capacity in the glory of reducing other people to a still more abject subjection. This is the solution suggested in a peculiarly sinister passage in Nietzsche. If so, the people constitute themselves partners of a common good of a false and inhuman sort. So far as the illusion of service to a state standing above its members encourages such false values, it is practically mischievous as well as theoretically false. Where an organized society has a " good " opposed to the summed up gain and loss of its component members, it is either that some of those alleged members are treated merely as instruments external to the body they share or that the good is a false good, cheating even those that partake of it.

When we speak of a good we mean a good supposed to be realized in the life of society itself. So far as any society subserves ends beyond its own limits, as, e.g. a state may be said to owe, and even to perform, a service to civilization, different principles of course apply. It may be right and good for a state like Belgium to risk all in such a case, but even here there is no final distinction between the duty or well-being of Belgium and of the Belgians as Belgians.

ing. Such a term is "a common self " or "the general will," suggested by a particular unity which connects the parts of a personality and which is precisely the form of unity that different persons do not achieve and into which they cannot enter. Such a term as "mind," "soul" or "spirit," though not satisfactory, is more appropriate, if so used as to suggest a collective character rather than a substantial unity. We can speak of the soul of a people, meaning thereby certain fundamental characteristics of their psychology which we believe to be widespread and important in the shaping of their social behaviour. We speak of the spirit of the times not inappropriately as a summary name for certain moral and intellectual tendencies, and generally the term "spirit" is appropriate for the relations of finite centres of intelligence each thinking, feeling and acting with reference to one another, and so linked together by mental and moral causation, just as physical structures are united by mechanical forces. But whatever terms we use, the rule of logic is simple. Our reasonings must always stand the test of substituting the thing defined for the definition. We must avoid importing into our defining term the associations which belong to it in another capacity. If we keep this rule before us, the terms which we use to describe society will have a less disturbing effect upon the progress of sociology. Thus, if we speak of a society as organic, we must not think of it as a great Leviathan, a whole related to individuals as a body to its cells. We must regard the organic as a genus into which animals and plants fall as species and society as another species. So considered, an organism is a whole constituted by the interconnection of parts which are themselves maintained each by its interconnection with the remainder. Its mutual determination is the organic character which any given structure may share in greater or less degree, a structure being organic in so far as this character prevails and otherwise inorganic. In its completeness the organic is an ideal. But actual societies have a touch of the organic character, some more and some less. It is on this character that social ethics depends. It is through this character that societies, like biological organisms, maintain their plastic adaptability, their power of adjustment to new circumstances, of repairing injuries, of resilience to strokes of fortune. It is by reference to this character that their development is to be measured. This principle is set at nought when society is so resolved into individuals that the character of the life which they share is left out of account. It is equally set at nought when its life is regarded as other than that which its members live in their dealings with one another. The happiness and misery of society is the happiness and misery of human beings heightened or deepened by its sense of common possession. Its will is their wills in the conjoint result. Its conscience is an expression of what is noble or ignoble in them when the balance is struck. If we may judge each man by the contribution he makes to the community, we are equally right to ask of the community what it is doing for this man. The greatest happiness will not be realized by the greatest or any great number unless in a form in which all can share, in which indeed the sharing is for each an essential ingredient. But there is no happiness at all except that experienced by individual men and women, and there is no common self submerging the soul of men. There are societies in which their distinct and separate personalities may develop in harmony and contribute to a collective achievement.

CONCLUSION

THE best and the worst things that men do they do in the name of a religion. Some have supposed that only supernatural religion could mislead. The history of our time shows that if men no longer believe in God they will make themselves gods of Power, of Evolution, of the Race, the Nation, or the State. In the name of such gods will they drench a continent with blood, and the youth will offer themselves up as willing martyrs. There is no double dose of original sin which established this worship in Germany. It is the product of a combination of historic causes—the long division of the people, their geographical situation, the national reaction against Napoleon, the achievement of union by military means, the fear of the Czardom, causing the acquiescence of the more pacific elements in militarism, the loss by emigration of those who would not tolerate the governing system. The idealized exaltation of the state supervened to reconcile the thinking classes and give them a creed justifying their dislike of humanitarianism. In Hegel's hands this creed had, as we have seen, its idealistic side, and events had to move before this could be shed, and the naked doctrine of Power be proclaimed by Treitschke. But the elevation of the state above men means at bottom the supremacy of Power. It is the natural creed of an aristocracy or a bureaucracy, as insistence on Personality is the natural creed of the people. Theories of politics or of conduct that live long and retain influence have something more than theory behind them. They appeal to powerful instincts and interests, and the Hegelian philosophy is no exception. It appeals to the instincts and interests of counsellors and kings, of privileged classes, of Property and Order. It plays on the fear of fundamental criticism, of the razor-edge of thought, of the claim of conscience to scrutinize institutions and ordinances. It appeals to the slavishness which accepts a master if he will give the slave a share of tyranny over others more deeply enslaved. It satisfies national egoism and class ascendancy.

It was by no accident that the Greatest Happiness Principle took root and flourished during and after the last great war that devastated Europe. The spectacle of the massive misery caused by Governments had its recoil. Men began to test institutions and ideas of life by their effect on the felt happiness and misery of millions, and they found in the " happy fireside for weans and wife " a truer measure of a nation's greatness than stricken fields and extended territory. To that view in essence we are returning to-day. Much has been learnt in the interval, and a modern thinker could not regard happiness crudely as a sum of pleasures, or divorce it from the mode of life which is its substance, or judge the well-being of a whole society by the contentment of a numerical majority. But the desire to arrest the misery of mankind will revive in double strength. Europe has undergone its martyrdom, millions in the service of false gods, other millions in resisting them. It will ask itself what is the true God and where the true religion. The answer, whatever it be, must rest on this truth, that the higher ethics and the deeper religion do not come to destroy the simplest rights and duties of neighbour to neighbour, but to fulfil and extend them. Great purposes, vast schemes, haunt the imagination of man, and urge him on to achievements without which life would be relatively poor and stagnant. But too often such purposes are built on foundations of human misery and wrong. It is the rarer insight which sees in the great good the comprehensive unity of all the little things that make up the life of the common man. The theory of the state is a case in point. The state is a great organization. Its well-being is something of larger and more permanent import than that of any single citizen. Its scope is vast. Its service calls for the extreme of loyalty and self-sacrifice. All this is true. Yet when the state is set up as an entity superior and indifferent to component individuals it becomes a false god, and its worship the abomination of desolation, as seen at Ypres or on the Somme. When it is conceived as a means to the extension of our duty towards our neighbour, a means whereby we can apply effectively and on the large scale what we know to be good in the simple personal relations of life, no such discord arises. The purposes of political action are no way narrowed, but purified and humanized. We learn to think of our political conduct in terms of the vast reverberation of consequences on thousands and millions of lives, great and lowly, present and to come. We cannot, indeed, ever adequately interpret great general truths in terms of the particulars which they cover. To give to vast social issues all their human meaning is beyond the power of imagination—an imagination which recoils even from the effort to appreciate the daily list of casualties. But the true progress of political thought lies in the cultivation of imaginative power. It insists on going back from the large generality, the sounding abstraction, the imposing institution, to the human factors which it covers. Not that it wishes to dissolve the fabric. Men must continue to build, and on deeper foundations and with larger plans. But there must be no slave buried alive beneath the corner stone. Or rather, the fabric is no building, but a tissue of living, thinking, feeling beings, of whom every one is " an end and not a means merely," and the value of the whole is marred if it requires the suffering of any single element. There is no lack of vastness in this design. It might rather be accused of vagueness, if it were not that it starts with the simple relations of man and man and bids each of us seek to realize in political conduct and through social institutions, on the widest scale and in impersonal relations, what we well understand in our private lives as "our duty towards our neighbour."

Political morality is not super-morality, setting ordinary obligations aside. It is morality extended and defined, stripped of the limitations of class or national prejudice, generalized for application in great impersonal organizations, the only thing that can save such organizations from becoming inhuman. It may be said that institutions and politics generally can do little to make individuals happy. That may be true, but they can do a vast deal to make individuals unhappy, and to cut off this great source of woe is no unworthy aim. That is why a sound political philosophy will always insist on the individual, the freedom which is his basis of self-respect, the equality which is his title to consideration, the happiness whereof "the tiny bowl is so easily spilt." It is not that our little lives are rounded in ourselves. On the contrary, if we find happiness anywhere, it is only in merging ourselves in some greater object. It is that if all objects worthy of effort may be considered as contributing to the advancement of mankind, this advancement, properly understood, goes not over the bodies and souls of individuals like a Juggernaut's car, but through their heightened activities and larger lives like a quickening spirit. Here precisely lies the issue between two views of the state. In the democratic or humanitarian view it is a means. In the metaphysical view it is an end. In the democratic view it is the servant of humanity in the double sense that it is to be judged by what it does for the lives of its members and by the part that it plays in the society of humankind. In the metaphysical view it is itself the sole guardian of moral worth. In the democratic view the sovereign state is already doomed, destined to subordination in a community of the world. In the metaphysical view it is the supreme achievement of human organization. For the truth let the present condition of Europe be witness.

APPENDIXES

APPENDIX I

HEGEL'S THEORY OF THE WILL

IN Lecture II the attempt has been made to elicit and criticize the main principles underlying Hegel's theory of freedom. A somewhat fuller explanation is here subjoined.

Hegel approaches the subject by a somewhat unfortunate analogy. The will is free in the same sense as matter is heavy. Gravity, he thinks, constitutes bodies. This in itself seems to be a mistake, partly of fact, but principally of definition. The expression "body has gravity" is a way of putting the fact that bodies, when otherwise unconstrained, move towards one another with a certain assignable acceleration. This statement by no means exhausts all that is known about bodies. If bodies were not known independently, that is, had no other attributes, we should not say that bodies had weight, but merely that weight exists. Whether all bodies do behave in the way referred to is a sheer question of empirical fact. But in any case gravity is not body, but is an attribute of body or, if it is preferred, a way in which bodies do behave. In the same way, if it is true that the will is free, it is certainly not in the sense that freedom is will or that will is freedom, but that freedom is a characteristic of will or an expression of the way in which will behaves. But will is not only freedom to Hegel, it is also thought. Will and thought are not two special faculties, but will is a specific mode of thought. It is thought as translating itself into existence,[1]

[1] In thinking, according to Hegel, I turn an object into a thought, stripping the sensible element from it and making it essentially and immediately mine. Thought penetrates the object, which no longer stands opposed to me because I have taken from it what was peculiar to it, which it had over against me. Similarly, in willing there appears at first an opposition between myself and my object, and in making a choice I make a distinction between a determinate end and my abstract potentialities. But this dis-

setting before itself an object with which it is in a manner identified. Ordinary language would recognize these expressions as having a loose metaphorical justification, but to Hegel they are the kernel of philosophy, and his conception of free will in particular will be found to depend upon taking them seriously. It is through his identification of the will with the system or totality of its objects that Hegel is able to speak of the will as determined only by itself, of the will as willing itself, and thus free from any other determination.

The development of this conception follows the ordinary dialectical process of Hegelian philosophy. We start with the conception of a will that is free in the sense of being quite indeterminate, so that it can choose anything and everything. But a will so indeterminate as this in fact chooses nothing and defeats itself. Hegel likens it to the anarchical movements of politics that want everything in general and nothing in particular. To escape from this barrenness we take refuge in particular objects or ends. But if the particular ends are isolated and disconnected they just miss that unity of action which distinguishes will. The truth then must be that, while the will sets a multitude of particular objects before itself, those objects must be united by some underlying principle.

It is in this unity of principle that Hegel finds what he calls freedom. The connection is by no means obvious,[1] but the drift of the argument may be gathered from the account of freedom as ordinarily, and in Hegel's view, falsely understood.[2]

tinction is after all my own, and the object, as I achieve it, belongs to me. It is mine when accomplished. The object is what I have done. There is a trace of my spirit in it.

[1] The argument is that since all the objects of the will fall under the same principle or have, as we might say, a function in one and the same system, they do not really limit the will as they seem to do, but express it in different forms. In seeming to limit itself, the will is expressing itself. This, according to Hegel, constitutes the freedom of the will, which is its substantive reality, as gravity is the substantive reality of body.

[2] It may be well to note the dialectical phases by which the conception of spurious freedom is reached. First, in § 8 we have what Hegel calls the formal opposition of the subjective to the objective. The will is something within me, contrasted with the outer world in which it seeks to realize its end. These particular ends form the content of the will, but, in adopting such ends (§ 10), the will does not fully attain its freedom. Its freedom is

This false conception emerges when the will stands contrasted as a distinct faculty or power of choice with the various impulses which direct it towards particular objects, each of which counts as distinct from and possibly opposed to others. The power of the will to choose between them is the kind of freedom which Hegel calls caprice (*Willkür*). And according to him it is at this point that the ordinary controversy as to freewill arises and on this plane that it is conducted. As long as the will is regarded as a bare potentiality, what Hegel calls something formal, standing over against impulses and promptings that proceed from elsewhere, whether within our nature or without it, you can argue with equal force either that it is determined or that it is undetermined. You can argue that it is determined on the ground that a mere potentiality, a bare form, has nothing within it to make it decide one way rather than another, whence you conclude that the propelling force must come from the impulse or from the presented object. You can argue equally that the will is undetermined because you can show that it can take up or drop any one of these objects and that what it can take up it can cancel, no matter what the strength of the impulse may be. In reality, according to Hegel, both arguments fail because both rest on a false conception of the relation of the will as a unity, or what he would call the universal, to its particular acts and impulses. The truth is that these particulars emanate from the universal character of the will itself. The will, therefore, does not stand over against the impulses which solicit it, but is itself the source of each movement in which it accomplishes and fulfils itself. The argument seems to ignore the distinction between impulse and will,[1] but again let us suspend criticism and try to follow the drift of the reasoning to the end.

implicit. It is in the will itself but it does not exist for, the will. That it should exist in this fuller sense, the will must realize itself as an object. There is a will operating whenever I adopt some definite end, and since there is a will operating there is freedom, but not, it would seem, the consciousness of freedom, not that organic connection between a particular end and a permanent underlying principle which constitutes self-determination. This is the stage which Hegel calls the immediate or natural will with its separate impulses and desires. The will stands above all these particular objects and can freely compare and choose between them. This brings us to the position examined in the text.

[1] Impulses antagonize one another, and one may calculate which impulse would bring the greatest satisfaction, but such calculation

To do this we must think of the will as expressing itself completely in a system of purposes all related to one another.

When it grasps this system as a whole it is said to exist for itself and to be its own object.[1] The meaning is that this system completely expresses the nature of the will and therefore for Hegel (here we get back to the ultimate identity of subject and object) *is* the will. True, there is always a distinction between subjective and objective, inner and outer aspects. Subjectively the will is the rational self-consciousness, objectively it is the rational system of ends. But to get the full " idea " of the will these aspects must be held together. The will therefore in willing its object is said to will itself. Thus for the will to be determined by its objects as a whole is to be determined by itself, and to be determined by itself is freedom. This is the substance of the entire argument, which culminates in the formula that the idea of the will is the free will which wills the free will.

This peculiarly difficult phrase proceeds directly from Hegel's identification of subject and object. Just as in the sphere of knowledge the mind, taken in its full concrete reality, *is* the system of the objective world which it knows, the knowledge itself being an aspect of the system, so we are to understand

again is mere caprice. According to Hegel, any identification of myself with some one impulse is a distinct limitation of the universality of the self, which is described in this section as the system of all impulses. This conception gives rise to another dialectical stage. The different impulses which issue immediately from the will are held to be good. On the other hand, as natural impulses, they are opposed to the conception of the spirit and have to be eradicated as bad. The truth is that they must be purified by being changed from their immediate or natural character and restored to what he calls their substantive essence, that is to the form in which they can play a part in the rational system which is the will.

The conception of happiness, involving some correlation of the different impulses, is a stage towards a rational life, but only a stage, because happiness lies in the individual human being, that is in his subjective feeling, so that what was to be universal turns out to be particular, something realized in particular people that is not an organic unity of all consciousness. The underlying truth (§ 21) is the self-determining universal, and this is will and freedom.

[1] And therefore infinite, for it turns back into itself like a circle, which, for Hegel, is the true representative of infinitude.

that in action the will *is* the system of accomplished purposes, the purposiveness of it being a part of that system. We are to conceive a system of activity penetrated throughout by a single principle or rather, we should say, engendered in all its variety of detail by a single principle, which requires infinite variety of forms in which to express itself, but a variety which by the interconnection of all its parts makes up an organic whole. This whole Hegel conceives as determined by nothing external to itself; any part of it may be regarded as determined by the will, but is in fact equally a determinant of the will. Its nature is to be a part of that will. So, in a sense, the will wills itself. Wherever you start, pursue the track of determination and you will come back to the point from which you started. This is the circle in which Hegel finds the meaning of infinitude, and that is why infinitude and self-determination are to him in the end the same thing.

In seeking to render the meaning plain to ourselves, we are constantly brought up against the initial difficulty of conceiving a will which wills itself. Surely when we will we are making, creating or bringing about something that does not exist ; something, whatever it may be, which is at any rate other than the act of making it. To avoid this fundamental difficulty and to discover, if we can, what substance underlies the Hegelian argument, let us put it, in more modern phrase, that the will and its object are conceived as an organic unity to be understood by the contrast in which it stands to that mechanical relationship which Hegel calls caprice. In this mechanical relationship there are a number of distinct and separate impulses, and a will apart from them all, moving above them and choosing now one and now another. In the organic relationship the different movements of the will, though distinct from one another, are emanations from one and the same principle. They could not exist without that principle, nor yet could the principle exist without them, nor indeed without any one of them, for each is an organic part of the whole.[1] Each impulse is, as it

[1] The only determinant of the will which Hegel contemplates is the object. If then he can show that the object emanates from the will, he proves on his presupposition that the will determines itself. It is to this that his demonstration is addressed. He does not consider the determinist point that the will with all its purposes (to admit that these emanate from within) arises out of antecedent conditions. But he is not really thinking of the will of an individual, but rather of the world spirit.

were, a bit of the will. Each bit of the will is determined by the will as a whole. Thus will is determined by will, that is by itself. And if, again, the will be considered as a whole which is determined by nothing external, but by its constituent parts, then similarly the will as a whole is self-determined. All its different objects are parts of a whole which hangs together and in which it is always expressing itself. This organic relationship is what Hegel understands by freedom, and so understood we have in this conception a system of action, the object of which is to maintain itself as a free system. This is what is expressed in the phrase " the free will which wills the free will."

Putting aside the phraseology, which depends on the impossible identification of subject and object, we have before us the conception of an organic or harmonious system of conduct. What precisely is a harmonious system ? It is one in which there are many parts, but so related that they all maintain or support one another. If we think of some occupation or some purpose which we deem desirable as a whole and which interests us in all its successive details, we have the model of a harmony of this kind. We take each step for its own sake because it is inherently attractive, and we also take it as a step in a journey, the end of which is equally attractive ; and thus there is at every stage a double motive, the immediate object for its own sake and also as contributory to the wider object which is intrinsically desired. If all life could be like that, it would be a perfect harmony and it would have nothing to do but to maintain itself. It would in fact be a self-maintaining system, such as Hegel contemplates, a system, that is, in which each part in effecting itself helps to give effect to the whole. Now the ideal to which moral purpose strives is a system of this kind, a harmony within the individual, a harmony as between all individuals—a unity, that is, in which each individual playing his own part, living a life which is desirable to him, is forwarding and consciously forwarding the life that is desirable for all mankind. In such a harmony, moreover, there would be perfect freedom, for the individual would be expressing himself unconstrainedly, and yet in expressing himself and by expressing himself, would be serving the requirements of the whole. But the freedom would be possible only because there is harmony and it would be truer to say that in such a system it is the will to maintain harmony than that it is the will to maintain free will which is the vital principle.

This leads us to inquire further into the relation between freedom and harmony. What is really meant by freedom? Ordinary thought translates freedom as absence of constraint. Hegel takes freedom as self-determination. In a world where nothing stands alone, where every act or event is related to something from which it follows and which is said to determine it, it is clear that of the action of anything whatever that we can regard as a continuous object, that we can identify through successive moments, one of two things is true. Either that action is an action of the object itself, proceeding from the nature of the object, arising out of the state in which the object has been, and consisting in a further state of activity which is just what the object of itself becomes. In that case the object may be said to determine its own action, or, regarding the object as one through successive phases, that is, before the action and in it, we can speak of the object, if we will, as self-determined in its activity. The other alternative is that the object should be determined by something else acting upon it. Then we speak of it as constrained. In the purely physical world, ordinary thought recognizes this contrast between freedom and constraint. A lever may be said to move freely about its fulcrum. The law of gravity expresses the way in which two bodies move freely, the pendulum moves freely about its support, all in contrast to the way in which these objects would behave under the constraint of some external force operating upon them. It may be objected that no one of these bodies really moves of itself. The pendulum, for instance, is part of a system of forces. There is its point of support, the weight attached to the rod, the rod itself and the earth. Nevertheless the swing of the pendulum is the resultant of just this particular system of forces acting without constraint by others, and that absence of constraint is what is meant when it is said that the pendulum swings freely. That particular system of forces determines of itself, and without the impingement of any other forces, just the particular set of motions which we discover. On the other hand, if the pendulum is deflected by a magnet, a push or a catch, a new force intervenes by which it is constrained. The whole system, including this new force, again may be said to act freely if no other intervenes. But in every case freedom from some external constraint will mean determination by the forces that are within the particular object or system of objects, which is the subject of our discourse.

When we come to the action of living things, and in particular to the will, we still mean by freedom primarily this same thing, the determination of the act by the character of the living thing itself, in particular of the will, as against determination by anything other than itself. What I choose to do at this moment, if I choose freely, expresses the character of my will at this moment. True, some external thing may be the stimulus which sets the will in motion, and it is because I see the rose perhaps that I have the impulse to bend down and smell it or pick it. But the rose does not constrain me, rather it suggests an experience, and the fact that I think of that experience as pleasing is a circumstance of my inner nature and precisely the circumstance which expresses itself in my impulse. In so far as any external object does constrain me and in so far as it awakens in me that which I cannot resist, I am deemed, and rightly deemed, not to be free, to be a slave to the external thing. Or again, if this craving is, as rightly regarded it should be regarded, rather inner than outer, then I am a slave to one of my impulses and my will is not free. If, on the other hand, knowing quite well what I am about and what was coming from my act, I perform that act with a view to that result, then that act is an expression of my will. It is unconstrained by anything external, not merely to myself, but to my will, and my will is free.

But there is a further sense in which the will is free which does not apply to material things. Given the pendulum duly attached to its support and raised from the vertical and then set free, that is, released from all external constraint, the result will be uniform and certain. The pendulum will swing to and fro. Each swing is determined accurately by the past swing. The movement of each moment is determined by the configuration of the preceding moment. Thus the mechanical system, though free from external restraints, is never free from its own past.

The question of the freedom of the will morally considered has been whether the will can ever be said to be free from its own past. The answer to this must be in a sense negative and in a sense affirmative. There is no reason to doubt that what my will is now is something which has come out of all that it and that I have been ; and there is no ground for assigning at any point a breach of continuity. The difference between the will and the mechanical system is this. The will looks towards that which is coming out of it ; it is in a sense determined not by the past but by the future ; and yet that future is something which it itself creates. It creates the end by which it is itself determined. The fact that the will creates this end is itself the determining point of its activity. It is in this sense that the will is self-determined in a way in which nothing that is mechanical can be. The pendulum does not swing because it wants exercise or because it wants to get to the other side. It swings as a result of the forces that are working within the system to which it belongs. The will, it may be said, also operates in accordance with the forces working within it, but these forces are such as to create a result which it foresees and it is because they create this result that the will acts as it does. The consequence is that there is no limit to the self-determination of the will. If at any point in the course of its activity something indicating a different result, previously unforeseen, emerges the will is able to adapt itself to this new circumstance. There is no fact bearing upon the issues of its action which the will is constrained by its past to omit. The past has made it what it is, but what it is is something looking to the future, determining its movements by their relation to the future. Self-determination in general then means the operation of an object in accordance with its own character and the self-determination of the will in particular, its operation in accordance with the character of a creative impulse. Unconstraint and self-determination are thus two expressions for the same thing, the one negative and the other positive.

With this definition in mind, we can easily recognize that the harmonious system of conduct, or let us say the harmonious will, is also in its inward relations a free system and a free will. Let us think of such a system as produced in each part by a several and separate act of will. Each act expresses itself, or rather in each act as it is at the time and in the relations appropriate to the action, the will is expressing itself without let or hindrance from other acts or relations of the will. Not only without let or hindrance from them, but furthered, maintained and supported by them, while also yielding to them furtherance and support. We think of the will in each act as looking not only towards the act itself, but also towards the entire system of willing of which it is a part, as expressing itself in both relations and finding the two relations harmonious. In such a harmony each deliverance of the will is free, that is it is unconstrained by any other deliverance of the will. Now for any single act of will there is just the same freedom if it is performed without any consciousness of relation to the will as a whole, for it is performed without constraint and it is therefore self-determined. But the will as a whole can only have freedom within if its purposes harmonize, otherwise there is constraint of some of its deliverances by others and they cannot all be free. In particular, if the permanent character of the will, its main tendency or its general principle, is in conflict with and overbears its own impulse in some particular case; the result in that case is not freedom but constraint. Here it would seem that Hegel would rejoin, "Yes, but the constraint that you speak of as exercised by the will in one particular relation is a constraint exercised by the will as a whole upon the will at a particular moment, that is, a constraint exercised by the will upon itself. Thus it is still self-determination and therefore it is freedom." But if this argument is advanced, it must be rejoined that self-determination so interpreted is by no means a satisfactory definition of freedom. If there is self-determination without harmony, what results is that the particular act or phase of will may be to any degree constrained, deflected, inhibited in its self-expression by the will as a whole, or, if the phrase be preferred, by the unifying principle of the will. Thus instead of the freedom of each several act of will we may have an absolute constraint exercised by the whole upon the parts. If it be said that this at any rate leaves the general principle of the will free to express itself, it must be replied that all we know of this principle is that it consists in the complete domination of all distinguishable phases or acts of will. The will is not willing itself, but against itself. Thus, in place of the free will that wills the free will, we have the conception of the will that in its freedom wills the total subordination of will ; or, in other words, freedom without harmony turns out to be constraint, the subordination of the particular to the universal. On the other hand, the freedom which is found in harmony is the expression of each particular phase of will in its own nature, and it is only if order and harmony are assumed to be convertible terms that it is possible to lay down a priori that a system dependent on a single principle is at once self-maintaining and free. The truth is that the Hegelian conception of freedom really points towards an idea of harmony which Hegel himself does not seem to have appreciated.

Freedom in the sense of absence of internal friction could be realized in a completely harmonious order of conduct but in no other. But free will, as Hegel uses the expression, is simply will which carries through a single principle, that is really a self-disciplined will—disciplined in accordance with law and custom —and wherever he uses the term "freedom," the term "self-discipline" should be substituted to make sense of his argument. In place of the will that wills the free will we should speak of the disciplinarian will that wills the subordination of all those partial impulses. In this conception there is, if you like, freedom for the central principle of the will, but for that alone—a freedom like that of James I's free monarchy, which meant that the monarch was free to do what he wished with every one else. It follows quite clearly from Hegel's view that the bad will is not free, but on this point he must be charged with distinct inconsistency, for when he comes to deal with the responsibility for wrong-doing (§ 139, p. 183) he explicitly maintains, as against the view that evil is necessary, that "the man's decision is his own act, the act of his freedom and his guilt." But it is clear that in his usage of the terms this could only be true if wrong-doing were the universal principle of the will. Hence the man who acts wrongfully is not free ; he is expressing caprice (*Willkür*) and has no freedom. Hegel cannot have it both ways. Either freedom means self-determination expressing itself in the choice between good and bad, and therefore as distinctly in the bad as in the good. In that case man as a moral agent is free, but free to do both ill and well. Or, freedom means subjection to the discipline of the goodwill. In that case man is free when he does good, but is not free to choose between good and evil.

To sum up, Hegel's conception of freedom depends upon a confusion between two distinct conceptions. On the one hand there is freedom in the sense of self-determination in any act of the will which is carried through without restraint. Freedom in this sense does not depend on any positive relation between one purpose and another, but might be realized in an isolated act without conscious relation to any other. On the other hand, in the will as a system of purposes there is freedom from any internal check or restraint only if all these purposes are in harmony. Hegel's account seems to fuse these conceptions, taking control of the partial purpose by the whole to be self-determination and therefore freedom, without postulating harmony as a condition. Now in the conception of a moral order which is a perfect harmony the freedom of the whole is the gathered fruit of the freedom of each part. In self-determination without harmony there is for the partial manifestations no freedom but subjection, and for the governing will no ideal of freedom but only of order. To speak of the latter conception in terms only applicable to the former is the fallacy that runs through all Hegel's theory of the law and the state.

APPENDIX II

THE THEORY OF THE ABSOLUTE

Dr. Bosanquet's theory of the state is so intimately bound up with his general theory of Reality, that a discussion of his social philosophy can hardly be complete without some reference to his conception of the Absolute as contained in the two volumes of his Gifford Lectures, to which reference has several times been made in the preceding chapters. Indeed, for him the state seems in a manner to be the medium, it is certainly one of the media, by which the individual comes into contact with the Absolute. The Absolute is sovereign Lord, but the state is its vicegerent here and now. What then is the Absolute and how is it related to our lives?

The Absolute is that in which all contradictions are reconciled. But this definition really includes two characteristics which are perfectly distinct. By contradiction is meant, in the most natural and straightforward sense of the term, logical contradiction. It is clearly true, but it is also a platitude, to say that logical contradictions cannot exist in reality. If the Absolute then is an expression for reality as it is in its completeness, it is certain that within it there can be no contradictions. Whether we should say on this point that within it contradictions are reconciled is not so certain. Contradictions really exist in the world of partial knowledge, and it would be truer to say that they must necessarily be reconciled, that is, resolved away, in complete knowledge, while in reality they cannot really exist. However, to let this verbal point pass, it is clear that in the Absolute all elements of reality which as partially or separately known to us are imperfectly understood, and thus give rise to apparent contradictions, are so related by underlying principles of connection as to constitute a consistent whole. All this is little more than platitude, put it as we may.

But there is a second meaning of contradiction—practical

contradiction, conflict, opposition, under which, in general, pain, misery, evil and destruction may be grouped. That there exists any being, call it what we will, in which all such conflicts are reconciled, is a much more doubtful proposition. It can by no means be regarded as a postulate of thought, as the first proposition may be, and I suspect that its plausibility depends upon an unconscious transition from the first meaning to the second. That contradiction in this second sense may be somehow reconciled in undoubtedly the aspiration of the religious consciousness, but its realization is not a fundamental postulate of philosophy. What has here to be asked, however, is whether Bosanquet's Absolute does in fact provide any such reconciliation ; and if so, at what cost to our moral and religious ideas ? Bosanquet's view is that the Absolute is perfection and that all the content of our experience, whether we call it good, bad or indifferent, would be found, if we had full knowledge, to play its necessary part in this perfect scheme. What we have to ask is in what way evil, pain and conflict and destruction can have a part to play in a perfect scheme. One answer would be that these things are necessary incidents of a process in which some life is evolved or some plan being worked out so good and glorious that if we could understand it all, we should deem it worth the cost. This conclusion, however, is expressly barred by Bosanquet, who refuses to conceive the Absolute as the realization of a purpose. In point of fact, the conception of purpose is only applicable if we think of it as operating upon material which is given to it, or at least under conditions by which it is so limited as to make the suffering and destruction necessary to the completeness of its work. At bottom this is why Bosanquet rejects the conception of purpose. It cannot characterize the whole. But he does not seem to consider the alternative that the whole might be something in which the element of purpose is that which we really value, so that the ultimate success of this purpose would reconcile us to the cost.

Rejecting purpose, we have to be satisfied with a world which is not going to be any better than the world of our experience but is of one tissue with it, only complete. We might perhaps value such a world if we could think of it, for example, as a kind of living organism, as an organic unity. But the characteristic of an organic unity is that it maintains the parts by which it is constituted. Thus, if there is destruction and pain within the organism, it is either because the organism is acted upon by foreign bodies or because it is in some way imperfect. The universe is not acted upon from without, and if organic at all, must be imperfectly so. But the difficulties that arise here are not relevant, for Dr. Bosanquet's Absolute is the very reverse of organic in its conception, being quite indifferent to the permanent welfare of the units, spiritual beings, selves, which go to make it up. The life of any one of them may end in disruption and despair, and yet reconciliation is supposed to be found in the Absolute. The Absolute thus presented is something utterly inhuman, without bowels of compassion. It is below the moral categories, as everything that pretends to be above them invariably is.

But if the Absolute is neither purpose nor an organism, what is it ? Bosanquet answers that it is perfection. It is not good and it is not evil strictly, for we judge things good or bad by reference to the perfection of the whole. Can this perfection give us any reconciliation ? The answer is that it may reconcile logical contradictions, but for that we need no conception of perfection but simply of reality, or, to phrase it better, of reality thoroughly understood ; but that there is only one way in which conflict, pain, evil and ills can be said to be reconciled either with one another or with any scheme or order to which our emotions and admiration and satisfaction can attach themselves, and that is by showing that they are necessary steps in the fulfilment of some purpose which we regard as fully adequate to the heavy cost which they represent. If reconciliation means anything other than this, the meaning should be specified. There is no suggestion that it means anything else except the overcoming of contradictions, which has been shown is a different concept not to be surreptitiously identified with the ideal in question.

Certain passages in Bosanquet suggest a possible line of reply approaching more nearly to the ordinary ethical and religious view of reconciliation. An evil, it may be said, is transformed into something which is not evil and perhaps even good by the way in which we take it, by our fortitude, by our resignation, by our accepting it as the burden which we must bear for others, and so on. Now, it is true that by our attitude an evil may be modified and in some respect turned to a good account ; but, though modified, the evil is not cancelled. If the sufferer does not resent it for himself, we resent it and are right to resent it for him. The finer his attitude, the stronger should be its appeal to us onlookers as a flagrant wrong which man, or nature, or an Absolute, if you will, has imposed on a being who is showing himself worthy of better things. In the individual sufferer who uses his suffering nobly there is reconciliation, but it is precisely not in the Absolute that this reconciliation is achieved. It is in reality ıs a whole that the wrong remains, and so far as it is overcome it is the work of the human spirit operating in reality.

Lastly, if we really need pain and evil as a substratum for our good, then it may be true that the most we can do is to maintain a life of struggle. This cannot be attributed to the perfection of the Absolute, but to a deep-seated dissonance in the structure of things, which not only is not, but on this principle never could be reconciled. It must be added that if, as Bosanquet appears to maintain, effort cannot ever fundamentally improve this situation, then effort is fundamentally hopeless and discord is absolute. If, on the other hand, effort can make an improvement, then, though the discord is there, it is capable of mitigation and it becomes conceivable that through effort, conscious and active beings may achieve a life worth the pain and travail. It is in the notion of such a life, either here or hereafter, either for others or for ourselves, that every one who has not argued about the issue, but felt it, looks for that which may repay the terrible cost of human suffering.

INDEX

Absolute, 17, 18, 19, 20, 24, 116
    Theory of the, 150, 151, 152, 153
Alexander, Professor, 53
Aristotle, 60, 73

Body, 53
Bosanquet, Dr., 18, 19, 21, 22, 37, 38,
    40, 41, 42, 43, 44, 45, 46, 47, 50,
    51, 53, 54, 55, 56, 57, 58, 59, 60,
    61, 69, 70, 73, 74, 75, 76, 77, 78,
    79, 80, 81, 82, 83, 84, 85, 86, 94,
    102, 103, 104, 105, 106, 107, 108,
    109, 110, 111, 112, 113, 114, 115,
    116, 120, 123, 150, 151, 152, 153
    Philosophical Theory of the State, 22,
    40, 50, 56, 74, 94
    Principle of Individuality and Value,
    19, 69, 79, 82
    Social and International Ideals, 21,
    59, 94, 106, 120
Bridges, J. H., 115

Church, the, 88, 89, 90
Clark, Mr. William, 24
Common Aim, 123
Common Good, 123
Comtists, 115, 116
Cynics, 72

Ethics, 11, 46

Force, 74, 77, 122
Freedom, 26, 31, 32, 33, 34, 35, 36,
    37 ,39, 40, 59, 60, 139, 141, 145,
    147, 148
    Moral, 43

Gravity, 138

Green, T. H., 24, 83, 96, 99, 118, 119
    120, 121, 122, 123, 124, 125
    Principles of Political Obligations,
    116
Goethe, 98

Harmony, 36, 46, 47, 143
Hegel, 17, 18, 20, 21, 23, 24, 31, 32, 33,
    34, 35, 36, 37, 38, 39, 40, 56, 62,
    64, 65, 68, 69, 79, 87, 88, 95, 96,
    97, 98, 99, 100, 101, 102, 103,
    118, 134, 138, 139, 140, 141, 142,
    143, 144, 147, 148, 149
    Philosophy of History, 17, 20
    Philosophie des Rechts, 20, 23, 24,
    38, 79, 87, 96
Hegel's Theory of the Will, 38, 138
Höffding, Professor, 15
Humanity, 115, 116
Hume, 63

Ideals and Facts, 14, 18
Idealistic Social Philosophy, 41
Individual, 51, 66, 67

Kant, 100, 101

Law, 26, 32, 38, 92, 114, 149
League of Nations, The, 25, 106, 107,
    116
Lycophron, 60

Marx, Karl, 24
Mazzini, 106
Metaphysical Theory of the State, the,
    18, 21, 73, 76, 117, 118, 122, 130
Mill, 42

9 780415 557863